The Quest for Quality

SRHE and Open University Press Imprint
General Editor: Heather Eggins

The Quest for Quality

Sixteen Forms of Heresy in Higher Education

Sinclair Goodlad

The Society for Research into Higher Education
& Open University Press

Published by SRHE and
Open University Press
Celtic Court
22 Ballmoor
Buckingham
MK18 1XW

and 1900 Frost Road, Suite 101
Bristol, PA 19007, USA

First Published 1995

A catalogue record of this book is available from the British Library.

ISBN   0 335 19350 1 (pb)   0 335 19351 X (hb)

Library of Congress Cataloging-in-Publication Data
Goodlad, Sinclair.
    The quest for quality : sixteen forms of heresy in higher
education / by Sinclair Goodlad.
        p.   cm.
    Includes bibliographical references and index.
    ISBN 0–335–19351–X. — ISBN 0–335–19350–1 (pbk.)
    1. Education, Higher—Aims and objectives. 2. Quality (Philosophy)
3. Education, Higher—Great Britain—Evaluation. I. Title.
LB2322.2.G66   1995
378′.001—dc20   94–41405
                                                                   CIP

Typeset by Graphicraft Typesetters Ltd., Hong Kong
Printed in Great Britain by St Edmundsbury Press Ltd,
Bury St Edmunds, Suffolk

For Inge and Emily

Contents

Acknowledgements

As in most adventures in ideas, one stands on the shoulders of others, rather than looks over walls on one's own. My first debt is to the Higher Education Foundation (HEF), of which I was founding secretary in 1980, and the two chairmen with whom I worked, Roy Niblett and John Dancy. Many of the ideas elaborated here were first tried out on the trustees of the HEF: any lustre they may have undoubtedly comes from the refining fire of their criticism; any blemishes that remain are almost certainly the result of my not listening to good advice!

The Center for Higher Education Studies at the University of California, Berkeley, helped me greatly by affording me time and opportunity to study in 1983 and in 1986. I owe special debts of gratitude to Martin Trow, Sheldon Rothblatt and Janet Ruyle.

Between 1985 and 1987, I served as Secretary of the Voluntary Sector Consultative Council (VSCC), which represented the interests of eighteen church colleges in their dealings with the (then) National Advisory Body for Public Sector Higher Education and the Department of Education and Science. I am grateful to my quondam colleagues of that time for the opportunity to explore how some of the ideas here examined take effective institutional form. Subsequently, through work with the Council for Church and Associated Colleges (CCAC), I have had many opportunities to sustain the debates begun within the VSCC. So many, varied and fruitful have been the opportunities to chew the cud with principals and teachers in those colleges that it would be invidious to mention names other than that of the chairman of the CCAC, Gordon McGregor, who has been unfailingly supportive both personally and professionally.

My debts to Imperial College are also too numerous to list in detail. By their boundless enthusiasm and searching questions, my students have been a constant stimulus. My admiration for the selfless energy and cheerfulness with which they have acted as tutors in the scheme known as 'The Pimlico Connection' (see Chapter 4 below) has sustained my commitment to the idea of study service. John Hughes, himself a former tutor, has helped to spread the idea to some 180 other UK higher education establishments. Pat Kerridge typed a draft of this book with her usual speed and accuracy.

It has been a special privilege to run courses on university teaching methods with colleagues at Imperial College. Particularly valuable has been the opportunity (afforded by my workshops on technical presentation) to hear about the work done by colleagues in other disciplines.

My enthusiasm for independent study brought me into valuable contact (as chief external examiner) with the School of Independent Study at the University of East London. It was tremendously invigorating to see in action ideas which elsewhere in the university system appear just as unrealized dreams.

The Society for Research into Higher Education has afforded many opportunities to try ideas out on colleagues. I am grateful to the SRHE and Open University Press for giving a first airing (in *Academic Freedom and Responsibility* edited by Malcolm Tight, 1988) to four of the sixteen forms of heresy here set forth. The comments of two anonymous referees also helped me greatly in building on the outline and the first draft of the book.

Inevitably, my wife Inge and daughter Emily have borne the burden of the grouchiness that writing always seems to engender.

Sinclair Goodlad
Imperial College

1

Introduction

Aims

We are faced with a paradox.

People in universities study a huge number of subjects from a bewildering number of often competing perspectives; yet the rhetoric of the current debate about quality seems to imply a unity of purpose and outcome that is at variance with common perception of the characteristically postmodern atomization of universities. Can sense be made of the sound and fury?

In approaching this question, the objects of this book are:

- to examine a number of issues concerning the basic stuff of higher education – curriculum, teaching methods, research – that go deeper than the administrative shell that is the usual focus of the quality debate;
- to propose a position concerning the nourishment of persons from which all those involved with higher education can comment on and criticize the activity, and with which they can examine their own basic assumptions;
- to offer some examples or case studies, mostly drawn from my own experience, in which broad issues regarding good practice can be earthed in particularities;
- to argue that the uncertainty endemic in most research procedures regarding the processes (means) of higher education, and the fundamental impossibility of achieving philosophical consensus regarding purposes (ends), points to the need for threshold procedures of quality monitoring (i.e. ones that identify *necessary* conditions of effective practice) rather than ratings-based judgements that imply, incorrectly, that agreement is possible about what is *sufficient*.

My hope is that this short essay will be of use to politicians, funders, administrators, teachers, students, potential students and their parents, as they debate what universities are for, and what can reasonably be expected of and from them.

The 'heresies' of the title, like theological heresies, represent exaggerations of one or other aspect of the proposed position which constitute undesirable distortions. The intention is not to identify candidates for potential burning (although the prospect does in some cases, I must admit, offer a grim satisfaction!), but rather to sharpen up the position to a point at which it may encourage, or discourage, agreement.

All arrangements for higher education imply moral values; indeed, universities reflect in microcosm our society's perception of itself. In postmodern society, that perception may seem to be one of total incoherence. Yet as a specialized form of social institution within the wider society, universities have lasted for 800 years. Many people who work in them have firm views about what it is right and proper that they should be and do. Although the temper of our time is against airing issues of fundamental concern (the preference being rather for the discussion of technique), persisting patterns and customs (mores) invite scrutiny from an essentially moral perspective, one concerned as much with ends as with means.

Likewise, all research which seeks to illuminate purposes and practices in higher education also implies moral values. If debate is to be well-informed, criticism of institutional arrangements for higher education, and the research which provides the evidence upon which criticism is based, should, therefore, contain some statement about the moral preconceptions involved. That is the fundamental thesis of this book.

At present, we lack the language in which such statements can be made: there is a gap between the rhetoric of higher education (which often proceeds at a level of high generality) and research (and subsequent administrative action), which concentrates on limited 'technical' issues. This book explores some 'middle axiom' questions in higher education, i.e. those which attempt to link pragmatic, operational questions to the principles and coordinating concepts which might constitute a consistent and systematic approach to higher post-compulsory education.

That there is need for some such systematic approach to higher education can no longer be doubted. The rain of issues concerning curriculum, teaching methods, research priorities and college organization can, of course, be tackled pragmatically, with the rationale for decisions being glossed over in basically political compromises. Both external issues (concerning what proportion of public funds should go to higher education compared to health, housing, foreign aid, defence etc.), and internal issues (concerning how funds devoted to higher education should be divided between the various competing interests within the system in general and in particular institutions) can more readily be approached in this way. The recent retrenchment in higher education in most developed countries has only served to highlight the absence of any coherent basis for decision-making about what can and should be done by whom, when, where and how; it has not, in fact, raised new questions, but has, rather, made more urgent questions which were there (unanswered) already.

Strategy and assumptions

First, it cannot be over-emphasized that this book is intended as the beginning of a debate, not its conclusion. It represents not a fixed position but rather one possible approach: as it were, 'notes towards a philosophy of higher education' rather than a fully articulated philosophy. Its style is that of 'thinking things out' rather than that of 'finding things out', although general ideas are rooted wherever possible in specific details.

Second, much of the discussion will be in the dangerous (because largely uninhabited) ground between scholarship, reflection and research. (The distinction between scholarship, reflection and research is examined in Chapter 5.) A systematic approach to higher education must combine philosophical consistency with political and psychological credibility: ideally, it must be accessible, intelligible and stimulating to those with, perhaps, neither the time nor inclination to delve into philosophy, psychology and sociology, and simultaneously to those who are specialists in these contributory (commentating) disciplines. If the book succeeds in starting a debate, it will have served its purpose; to this extent, the book represents an agenda rather than a completed project.

Third, the book is not a guide to specific action, although some suggestions or preferences are included. Rather it is an aid to criticism – of self and of others – much as literary criticism is a commentary rather than a prescription.

Fourth, the book is primarily about *education*, not just about learning: the distinction is fundamental and crucial. Learning can, does and should take place anywhere and everywhere by anyone at any time. Education, by contrast, implies planning, organization, choice, control, institutions. Learning can be either plan-less and spontaneous or disciplined by a plan of one's own making (research) or of someone else's making (training). Learning in all forms, from research to training, can and does take place in a multiplicity of institutional contexts: homes, factories, offices, hospitals, theatres, churches etc. A theory of education, and of higher education in particular, is necessarily a theory of institutions because it must tackle very difficult questions about what learning requires special arrangements (including specialized institutions) and what learning can best be achieved in institutions whose purpose is not primarily the advancement of learning. It is precisely because education is about institutions, about patterned sets of social arrangements (customs, mores) that it must ultimately be tackled as a moral issue – one as much concerned with ends as with means.

Fifth, it will be important throughout to keep in mind the distinction between functions and institutions (see Goodlad, 1983b: 84). Institutions and functions can be considered independently, and functions can be achieved under any one of a variety of institutional arrangements. For example, the functions of higher education might include, *inter alia*: research (concept formation, data gathering etc.); scholarship (the refinement of observation, interpretation, evaluation); consultancy (dissemination of ideas from 'thought organizations' to 'will organization' in Moberly's

(1949: 39) parlance); teaching (creating conditions for learning and the assessment of achievement); social development (fostering interpersonal skills and competencies, widening intellectual horizons among students); social service (provision of work of direct social utility, by staff or by students); transmission of culture etc. These functions are distributed with considerable variation among different types of educational institution. They are also distributed with even greater variation between other types of social institutions. Indeed, one recent commentator (Wooldridge, 1994) has suggested that the rising costs of universities and their slowness of response to changing market demands may result in their being rendered obsolete by more nimble agencies and institutions offering the services traditionally offered by universities but in a more accessible form.

Which functions require what institutions? A large part of the argument of this book will concern a humanistic perspective which offers a principle of selection – so that those functions assigned to the specialized institutions we know as universities can be seen to have a rationale: without such a rationale, one cannot begin to debate pragmatic questions.

Sixth, an important consequence of maintaining the distinction between functions and institutions is that it becomes possible to talk about higher, post-compulsory, education with a certain freedom from the constraints of current, institutionalized, practice. The intention here is not to ignore important differences between different types of institution, but rather to provide a basis for constructive commentary and criticism regarding the division of labour in and between universities within a framework that keeps in mind some of the fundamental ideals of our culture. Because the basis of this criticism is moral (implying assumptions about how such difficult issues as 'the good life' and 'the nature of man' underlie conceptions of education as contrasted with learning), rather than political (implying questions about who can be compelled to do what), there is always a danger of drifting off into a Utopian discourse about what 'ought to be' rather than a tough-minded recognition of 'what is'. It is for this reason that throughout the book there are examples of actual practice; what could or should be done is earthed in description of what has been done. Indeed, most of the examples I quote are ones in which I have been personally involved or of which I have had the opportunity for direct observation – not because these are in any way special or superior to other examples, but rather because they may help readers to adduce examples of their own.

Seventh, it would be indeed a megalomaniac endeavour to try to prescribe a formula for all forms of higher education. An important characteristic of the approach used in this book is that it involves *resistances* rather than prescriptions. The book offers a perspective from which it should in principle be possible to appraise any form of university practice – although for purposes of conviction and coherence I write only of what I know. Chapter 2, for example, begins by identifying both technical difficulties with some research approaches to higher education and the assumptions (articulated or not) that seem to underlie them. The effect of this approach may seem to be to sow doubt rather than to offer confident advice, to imply hesitation rather than to foster incisiveness. It is, however, extremely important to note that this very doubt, uncertainty, tentativeness is at the heart of what the book asserts should be institutionalized in university education. The very lack of intellectual certainty which criticism produces is, it will be argued, the basis of a moral position, and may, in fact, be seen as the primary claim of the university to a central place in contemporary life and culture, and to a certain freedom of action and thought that may otherwise be compromised (see Russell, 1993).

Chapters 3, 4, 5 and 6 examine respectively aspects of curriculum, teaching methods, research priorities and college organization, in which issues of moral value occur. 'Heresies' are listed which, like theological heresies, represent exaggerations of 'truth' in one direction or another: the difference here is that, because no definition of 'truth' is attempted, the 'heresies' are offered as assertions of types of certainty which are represented as illegitimate in the light of the dilemmas addressed in the book. In each area, preferences for action are offered which accord with the position that underlies the book.

Universities as key institutions in modern society

Universities have become the central institutions of modern civilization. Not only are they places in which all ideas that we take seriously are subjected to systematic scrutiny, but they are increasingly being seen as the institutions responsible for our society's rite of passage between youth and adulthood. Misguided notions of how they should fulfil these functions currently threaten their survival. If we hope to keep our universities, we need to be clear in mind about what they are *for*, and how we may rightly judge whether or not they do their job well.

All societies have ceremonies which signal in a public manner the movement of an individual from one status to another. Arnold van Gennep, the anthropologist who wrote the definitive study of these ceremonies in 1960, shows how young people typically leave their families and withdraw under the supervision of selected elders into a period of separation from the economic life of their societies. During this time, they learn how to take their roles as adults. These initiation procedures reach their climax through colourful ceremonies in which the young people are presented in public by the elders of the society, ready to take on their adult roles. Nobody who has seen a degree ceremony can doubt that it is a rite of passage of this type. Some degree ceremonies even have royal personages to preside over them and/or take place in cathedrals, and the elders of our society dress up in ritual paraphernalia that makes the costumes of some witch-doctors look positively dull.

Perhaps it is the very absence in other sections of modern society of any comparable rites of passage that makes those who feel the lack of them strive to study for a degree – not for the intrinsic satisfaction of doing so, nor for the enhancement of earning that it is assumed (often incorrectly) that a degree will bring, but rather as a necessary recognition of adulthood. There may be occupations for which a university degree as such is unnecessary, and in which the functions fulfilled by universities can be better supplied by other procedures and other institutions. The danger is that the symbolic load carried by degrees will put at risk (by overloading) one, but only one, of the institutions that perform this ritual function in our society.

The increased number of universities

For many years in the United Kingdom, there was an uneasy split between universities and polytechnics. Because the overlap between their functions was great, the distinction caused much confusion, particularly to students overseas who were thinking of coming here to study, and much understandable resentment in the polytechnics. In 1992, the distinction was abolished with the polytechnics becoming universities. All political parties are keen to see as many young people as possible pass through universities (the target at present is about one-third of the age cohort). Other young people will continue post-compulsory education in further education colleges which, like community colleges in many states in the USA, are increasingly taking on (through the process of 'franchising') some of the work of the universities. How are we to view this huge increase in the number of universities, and of colleges offering degree-level study?

The comparison with the USA is illuminating, because there we may see a possible shape of things to come. In the state of California, for example, there is a three-tiered higher education system consisting of the University of California with nine campuses (including Berkeley, Davis and UCLA) which teach to doctorate level, the California State University with nineteen campuses which teach to the masters level, and some fifty community colleges which teach both university preparatory courses and non-degree vocational courses. The California Master Plan, which has operated since 1960, provides for movement between these tiers through the process of credit transfer. Some students can start working for a degree at a local community college, combining study with remunerative employment and living at home to save costs. They can then, as it were, 'cash' their credits at one of the campuses of the California State University or of the University of California and complete their studies in full-time mode. Some 50,000 students per year exercise the credit-transfer option.

The need for change in the United Kingdom

The pattern of university study in the United Kingdom was until recently modelled on that of the ancient universities (Oxford, Cambridge, St Andrews), with three years of full-time study, usually involving residence away from home being the norm. The growth of the so-called 'redbrick' universities (Leeds, Manchester, Hull etc.) broke the pattern of residence, with many students living at home while they studied. The redbrick universities also pioneered courses more directly related to the needs of industry than those of Oxford and Cambridge. In the late 1950s, some distinguished regional technical colleges were upgraded to become colleges of advanced techno-logy, and soon after that were again transformed into the technological universities (Brunel, City, Loughborough, Surrey etc.). The Robbins uni-versities (East Anglia, Essex, Lancaster, Sussex, York etc.), founded in the mid-1960s following the recommendation for expansion of the Robbins Committee (1963), seem to have reflected the English nostalgia for Ox-bridge (indeed, they were strongly peopled by Oxbridge dons who became the founding fathers). Again, they emphasized residence away from home – and even in some cases (Lancaster and York) had 'colleges' within them. Stewart (1989) gives a succinct review of these developments.

Although the United Kingdom has the most efficient university system in the world in terms of graduations per member of staff (see Marris, 1986: 142), it is also an expensive system. Until recently, most UK students not only had their fees paid by the state but also received most of their main-tenance costs (through grants from local government). As I write, there is constant ferment, with the government trying both to increase access and to hold down costs. Any other political party, or combination of parties, taking over from the present government will have the same problems to face. The snowstorm of documents discussing possible accelerated degrees, changes to the length of the academic year and so forth will no doubt continue for some time to come.

Already there has been a massive growth in part-time study, and in the proportion of mature students (those over the age of twenty-three) in higher education; the Open University is now the largest university in the United Kingdom. Credit-transfer facilities, the 'franchising' of parts of university degree courses to colleges of further education, the need of even 'full-time' students to take paid employment to pay their way through university, the migration of students through such schemes as ERASMUS and SOCRATES, the arrival in higher education of students who have taken a diversity of GCE A-level syllabuses (e.g. in mathematics) and who may not represent the homogeneous cohort that university teachers have been used to, the rapid spread of National Vocational Qualifications – all these developments make the boundaries of universities increasingly fluid.

I mentioned rites of passage above because they represent a primitive (in the sense of archetypal rather than crude or undesirable) pressure to sus-tain an equation of higher education with a particular social function, even a particular form to that function. Certainly we need rites of passage and, in a post-Christian society, it is interesting to speculate on how appropriate rites are to be sustained and managed in a manner that is consonant with the secular nature of our society and simultaneously satisfying at a deep psychological level. But a quite separate question is how those values fundamental to our society which have hitherto been nourished and sustained in universities can be kept alive in what must, of economic necessity if for no other reason, be a different sort of national scene.

The quest for quality

One symptom of the current anxiety about how to proceed is the obsession with quality.

Some studies, such as those concerned with performance indicators, concentrate on institutional inputs and outputs (e.g. Cave *et al.*, 1988; Johnes and Taylor, 1990). Others examine processes, sometimes assessing the feasibility or otherwise of bringing to bear on university practices ideas drawn from total quality management in industry (e.g. Barnett, 1992; Ellis, 1993; Green, 1994). It is immensely important to achieve consensus about what is to be desired because, as Shattock (1994: Chapter 3), for example, has shown, decisions are taken (based on good or poor indicators of quality) that drastically affect the lives and fortunes of universities.

At one level, quality is easy to define: 'fitness for purpose' (Ball, 1985). But this definition leaves unanswered the question of what the 'purpose' of universities is; it also omits the notion that some universities may be 'better' in some way than others in the sense that the purposes they serve may be more comprehensive or more desirable than the purposes of their competitors.

It may be tempting to cut the Gordian knot by trying to establish *the* idea of a university or of higher education (see Barnett, 1990; Pelikan, 1992). But *de facto* there are *lots* of ideas of higher education embedded in the institutions now designated universities. Unless we are to have a thought police systematically touring them and closing down those that do not conform, we must articulate a way of defining and defending a *variety* of models of university.

Debate about quality is taking place worldwide (see Craft, 1992; de Rudder, 1994; Frederiks *et al.*, 1994; Neave, 1994). Much of the debate concentrates on the *form* rather than the content of university education. By contrast, this book tries to identify what universities could attempt to *be* and do.

Rivers of ink, and years of person-time, are currently being devoted to quality *assurance* mechanisms, often with no reference to what exactly is to be assured. One recent document (HEQC, 1993) asks universities to provide documents exemplifying policies and practices relating to quality assurance. These, it suggests, might include: undergraduate and admissions access policies; equal opportunities; credit accumulation and transfer; modularization; new course or programme design and approval; programme or course reviews; departmental reviews; resource allocation for courses and programmes; validation of other institutions' courses; franchise arrangements for courses or programmes taught off campus; postgraduate students' admission; students' work and progress; research students' supervision; student assessment and degree classification; examination appeals; external examiners' appointments; external examiners' reports; academic staff appointment procedures; academic staff probation; staff development and training; academic staff appraisal; academic staff promotion criteria; teaching and learning innovation; academic standards; interaction with accrediting bodies such as BTEC and professional organizations; the securing of students' views on academic matters; the securing of graduates' views on academic matters; the securing of employers' views on academic matters; Enterprise in Higher Education projects.

Being concerned with quality *assurance*, rather than quality *control*, most of these items concentrate on administrative procedures rather than on the stuff of the academic enterprise. What is not clear is how these procedures, without further exegesis of how they operate, can have any bearing whatever on the quality of what universities do. Indeed, some of the apparently approved items (such as modularization and Enterprise in Higher Education projects) seem to signify the first green shoots of what could become a new orthodoxy – with a fiscal (rather than, as in this book, conceptual) hunt for heretics!

Having reached, it seems, the (not unsurprising) conclusion that the provision of quality assurance documentation has not been very illuminating about what quality actually *is*, the Higher Education Funding Council England (HEFCE) issued a further document (HEFCE, 1993) concerning the actual *assessment* of the quality of education. To aid institutions in their self-assessments, the HEFCE offers a 'template' with six sections corresponding to the structure currently used by the Council to give institutions feedback following an assessment visit. The sections are: aims and curricula; students: nature of intake, support systems and progression; the quality of teaching and students' achievements and progress; staff and staff development; resources; academic management and quality control. Each section refers to 'evidence' that the Council will be seeking, yet there is *no indication at all* of how this 'evidence' is to be judged! It is difficult to think of a more threatening and anxiety-provoking procedure.

Even the distillation of these matters into four basic questions avoids any indication of what 'quality' could conceivably be. The document indicates (p. 7) that an assessor will seek to answer four questions:

a. Is there evidence of a systematic, self-critical approach within which the institution has: evaluated relevant issues; demonstrated, as far as possible, the quality of provision in the subject; and developed plans for the future?

b. If yes, has the Institution claiming excellence made a prima facie case that it is providing excellent quality education in the subject? . . .

c. If no, are there grounds for concern that quality may be at risk? . . .

d. What are the main issues arising from analysis?

The very absence of any guiding comments makes one anxious that there may be a *hidden* agenda, the presence, in short, of biases such as those discerned by Atkin (1987: 230) in a random selection of HMI reports on institutions offering initial teacher training. It is, however, a reassuring indicator of the pragmatic good sense that informs policy matters in British higher education that the Higher Education Funding Council of England and Wales commissioned a study of its own procedures which was carried out by the Centre for Higher Education Studies of the University of London Institute of Education (see Barnett *et al.*, 1994). This report rightly calls for clarification of the criteria and procedures to be adopted by a team visiting a university (para. 19).

For example, the report questions the heavy focus on observation of teaching *performance* in the procedures used by the teams that visit universities (p. 31), pointing out that procedures designed to foster responsibility among students for their own learning (such as problem-based or resource-based curricula) might be undervalued. In its recommendations, the report stresses that quality of *learning* should be the focus of concern.

Finding our bearings

While the proceedings of the HEFCE Quality Assessment Division may, unless great care is taken, degenerate into an unanticipated and unacknowledged witch-hunt, we nevertheless need *some* notion of what range of activities can properly be assigned to universities. The variety cannot be infinite. There are, and must continue to be, some guiding concepts that help us to decide individually and collectively what we want – not least because everything currently done in universities can be done in other ways through other agencies of society. This book attempts to meet that need. It offers a few thoughts regarding possible guiding principles in four key areas of university life. These are:

- *curriculum* because the selection of what it is *worth* learning in universities is not random;
- *teaching methods* because universities offer opportunities for the *acceleration* and enrichment of learning that one could otherwise do on one's own;
- *research* because some research can perhaps better be carried out *alongside teaching* rather than in other settings (such as research institutes or industrial laboratories);
- *college organization* because institutions are *ends* as well as means in the sense that they can encourage conviviality as well as meet social demands.

I state a position rather than justify it. This is because my concern is with ends as much as with means, with identifying matters in which one can say what *contradicts or confounds* one's intentions rather than with attempting to justify them by fine logic. I hope my use of the word 'heresy' in this regard will not cause dismay but will, rather, encourage debate at the level that is now needed.

2
Approaches to the Study of Higher Education

If one starts with the assumption that the primary aim of higher education should be to take individuals, teacher or taught, within it to the highest level of what is known or knowable within the limits of time, money and human capability, one immediately encounters the fundamental paradox mentioned at the beginning of Chapter 1. Within academic disciplines, there is often a fair level of agreement regarding what it is worth trying to find out; without such agreement, mechanisms of peer review (in awarding research grants, in selecting items for publication in learned journals etc.) would not be possible. There is also often substantial agreement (though with, perhaps, more vigorous dissent) about what it is worth trying to teach to students once a course of study has been established. There is, however, much less agreement about the appropriate division of effort between different fields of learning or about how much of what learning can or should be made accessible to whom. In short, debate within academic disciplines is highly developed and articulate; debate between representatives of different disciplines is primitive or totally lacking.

This is a serious matter; as Gibbons (1993), for example, has argued, it leads to the difficulty of extending the methods of evaluation of research from the lower to the higher levels of the research system, from the micro (or project) level to the macro (or programme) level.

In what language can one talk intelligibly and intelligently about higher education? It is not words that we lack; it is grammar. Research information about practically every aspect of higher education abounds; what seems, however, to defeat us is the task of organizing the items of information into a pattern (of choices and subsequent administrative action) that attempts to relate means to ends. Systematic justification is, of course, another matter. The argument of this chapter is that the very absence of such justification, the absence of even the possibility of such justification, points to the requirement for a basically moral position to be taken concerning the desirable form and content of higher education, one that relates what is proposed as good practice to some internally consistent tradition of discourse about ends and means.

All practice implies theory, whether the theory is articulated or not. Indeed, Argyris (1982) has emphasized that espoused theories may differ from theories actually in use, and Schön (1983, 1987) has sought to analyse the types of working theory used by reflective professional practitioners.

At the root of most theories are assumptions about what it is desirable to do. In articulate debate about the purpose of higher education, represented in research about it, such assumptions lurk near the surface. They are, however, often neglected in favour of attention to 'technical' issues (of research methodology, scholarly detail, implications for policy) which deflect attention from the basic moral dilemmas. The following examples will illustrate the point.

First, in historical studies of higher education, the choice of subject to examine inevitably implies a preference. For example, historical research often indicates the basic orientation in a preface, with the main writing moving on to substantive but 'technical' issues. Sheldon Rothblatt, the doyen of historians of higher education, writes, in *Tradition and Change in English Liberal Education*, as follows: 'I . . . am interested in the nature of the transmission of cultural values over long periods of time and in whether historical continuity can be expected of the collection of beliefs we sometimes call "tradition"' (Rothblatt, 1976: 9). Why? While one marvels at the subtlety and lucidity of the scholarship deployed, one longs for some indication of why the transmission of culture should merit such a rich study – not just as a technical question within the discipline of history, offering insight into the nature of the institutions examined, but also as commentary on the form the institutions now take. In fact, Rothblatt supplies this need in a later work (Rothblatt, 1993).

In a wide-ranging and brilliant analysis of the idea of 'liberal education in the English-speaking world', he elucidates the 'long and seductive' history of the idea, showing how in the practice of higher education as well as in its rhetoric, the idea keeps reappearing, often in strange disguises. The current debate in the United States and elsewhere about 'the canon' (of great works fit to be studied by young people) is one recent example. Often practice drifts so far from disciplined rationale that Rothblatt observes (with perhaps a hint of exasperation?): 'Taken in aggregate, or even singly, it is nearly impossible for one historian to find these extraordinarily time-consuming efforts to keep an old inheritance alive more than a suggestion of its former purpose and traits. Even the exact sources of inspiration for American experiments are hard to pinpoint' (Rothblatt, 1993: 51).

As with his earlier study of English liberal education, so with this more widely sweeping study, Rothblatt's intention is 'to use historical perspective to identify certain possibly unpleasant facts' (p. 61) and to show that 'ideas about liberal education have not "evolved", that is, developed over time from one form to another with some identifiable thread of continuity between them, but have interacted with other historical variables to produce quite different and even unrelated species' (p. 62).

It is towards the end of the essay that Rothblatt's reasons for being interested in the idea of liberal education emerge. He draws on one definition of liberal education as 'a broad understanding of human nature, society, and institutions, accompanied by a critical capacity to make choices and distinctions and to exercise, where necessary, a responsible independence of mind.' After warning against turning ideals into idols, he notes how easy it has become to divide proficiencies from personality and to lose sight of the historical ideal of civilizing oneself through liberal education – an ideal that, he concludes (p. 73), 'is not all that bad.' In short, the magisterial historical scholarship is fittingly shown to be servant to a wider, basically moral, purpose.

Some other studies which are rooted in history are explicitly polemical. For example, Minogue's *The Concept of a University* (1973), which traces universities back to their medieval origins, and Nisbet's *The Degradation of the Academic Dogma* (1971) both assert a particular view of the university based upon a reading of the history of universities. Both books are conservative in orientation, seeking to reassert a view of universities as properly maintaining a certain distance from 'the world' in order to maintain a form of disciplined consciousness which both produces and requires a higher specific type of social institution. In both cases, the richness of material and force of argument deployed is compelling; but ultimately, one's judgement of their theses depends upon what one believes it is worth trying to achieve (or preserve). Through the pursuit of 'relevance', we may indeed be in danger of destroying social institutions which have survived the changes and chances of eight centuries of this fleeting world, albeit with different emphases and varying functions at different periods of their history. But analyses of the origins and special social and intellectual characteristics of universities do not, ultimately, add up to a defence of them. Minogue's study, which is 'an attempt at the philosophical exercise of describing the identity which makes universities distinct from other organs of instruction' (Minogue, 1973: 225), succeeds, like the best philosophy, in pointing up areas of choice; it does not, however, offer a justification of the identity which it portrays.

A second type of study, phenomenological in orientation, revisionist in historical method, would see Minogue and Nisbet as, at best, hopelessly nostalgic and, at worst, as knowing or unknowing defenders of vested interests. Following the Marxist interest in cultural reproduction and the maintenance and extension of hegemony by already powerful groups, a growing corpus of studies seeks to demonstrate how the form and content of education, including higher education, preserve the status quo by controlling access to highly remunerated or influential posts and/or by providing legitimation through their curricula of existing dispositions of power and privilege (see Young, 1971; Bowles and Gintis, 1976; Bourdieu and Passeron, 1977; Sarup, 1978; Sharp, 1980). There is undoubted force in the arguments deployed – and abundant corroborative evidence from the figures of recruitment to higher education which, despite significant reforms since the Second World War, show in the United Kingdom, at least, a massive imbalance in favour of the offspring of the higher social classes (see Halsey

et al., 1980; Warren-Piper, 1981; Edwards, 1982; Kerckhoff and Trott, 1993).
Criticism of the revisionists usually centres on the accuracy, or lack of it, of
their historical work and the validity of their interpretations (see Ravitch,
1977). Far more interesting, however, is the relative absence in much Marxist
writing of positive descriptions of any serious alternative to existing arrangements. Marxist alternatives have, of course, been propounded (see Pateman,
1972); but Bowles and Gintis, (1976), as critics of existing arrangements,
stop short of offering scenarios. Critical study as a method of uncovering
interests typically ends precisely where one would want the story to begin.

A third type of study, interested, like the phenomenologists, in who gets
what from higher education, is that of economic theorists, of whom Rich-
ard Freeman in *The Overeducated American* (1976) is a good example. Freeman, in this and in other studies, shows with considerable lucidity and
massive evidence the economic costs and benefits of study to students and
to others. Financial benefits to be enjoyed from higher education obviously
depend crucially on the condition of the labour market. From the late
1970s to the time of writing the expected lifetime earnings of graduates
compared to non-graduates have been significantly eroded. If one takes the
view that higher education is a 'positional good' (i.e. one to be enjoyed, the
more if it distinguishes those who have it from those who do not), this is
bad news indeed. Indeed, one popularizer of Freeman's evidence calls her
book *The Case Against College* (Bird, 1975) and argues that parents and their
aspiring student offspring might seek better forms of investment than higher
education!

What is obvious, and Freeman readily admits this, is that the plotting of
earnings profiles and so forth tells one nothing about the intrinsic
satisfactions both of studying at college and of the knowledge that is acquired. What economic studies of higher education do, perhaps, serve to
demonstrate is that students would be unwise to see higher education primarily as a 'positional good'; indeed, in his seminal study *The Social Limits
to Growth* (1977), Fred Hirsch demonstrates the folly of pursuing *any*
positional goods in society. The greater the number of people that have
degrees, the less valuable will having a degree be to any individual. 'Pecking
orders of institutions will become more marked, and social imbalances will
continue but with different institutional expression.' Hirsch's analysis usefully draws attention to the intrinsic satisfactions of study; with his emphasis,
the notion of anyone being 'over-educated' becomes ridiculous.

There is a difficulty with studies of the economic consequences of higher
education; granted that there is social imbalance in recruitment to higher
education, may it not be that any persisting economic advantage of having
acquired a degree is more a consequence of parental ambition, lifestyle,
contacts and so forth, rather than a direct consequence of study? Or, as a
third of the age-cohort pass through some form of higher education, economic advantage may go to those who obtain a certain *sort* of degree (or
one from a certain sort of – prestigious – place). We can, of course, never
find out, because any controlled experiment would be impossible to carry

out. Comparative studies, a pale substitute for controlled studies, already suggest that there are significant differences in economic life-chances for graduates of different types of higher education institution in the United Kingdom (see Harland and Gibbs, 1986; Boys *et al.*, 1988; Brennan and McGeevor, 1988). Current advocates of a graduate tax seem to underplay this disturbing issue.

It is a similar technical difficulty that vitiates the fourth type of study to be considered: so-called 'impact' studies of higher education. A distinguished line of scholars has attempted to measure the changes in knowledge and attitudes which result from the experience of college (see Pace, 1941, 1979; Jacob, 1957; Chickering, 1969; Feldman and Newcomb, 1969; Astin, 1977). Although complex sampling techniques and massive samples are used, (often running to 250,000 students a year), there is ultimately no way in which these studies can separate out the effects of maturation on students' beliefs and attitudes; nor can the studies eliminate the effects generated by the choice by students of certain types of college and the selection by faculty of certain types of students.

That college has *some* effects on the attitudes, knowledge and beliefs of students cannot be doubted; but it is beyond the capacity of educational research to demonstrate what this is. Although the 'impact' studies have the commendable object of illuminating what goes on in higher education (and although the questionnaires are highly intelligent catalogues of likely effects), we are once again left without guidance from research about the whys and wherefores of higher education, about the relationship of means to ends.

Many of the most readable studies of higher education are valuable because they do not force on to the organic phenomenon they discuss any 'scientistic' framework of observation (which may miss the most important items), but rather illuminate the type of judgement that has to be made and the process by which judgements are reached (see Annan, 1963; Kerr, 1963; Bailey, 1977; Parlett and Dearden, 1977; Bok, 1982; Becher, 1991). Even studies which offer models (a framework for decision-making) are often most readable when they appeal primarily to the reader's direct experience and judgement rather than attempting spurious types of measurement (see Becher and Kogan, 1980).

To have criticized the methodological weakness or unarticulated moral assumptions of some historical, phenomenological, economic and 'impact' studies is not, of course, to condemn them. Like the best forms of academic study (and I deliberately selected leading examples), they offer illumination by limiting the field of discourse. To achieve precision and coherence, each type of study emphasizes one or another aspect of education which we neglect at our peril; but, ultimately, for the research data to be illuminating, one has to exercise a judgement. That judgement has two parts: one a view about individuals, the other a view about social institutions.

In any systematic approach to higher education, a view about individuals (a doctrine of man) must precede a judgement about institutions, because institutions are social arrangements designed to achieve human purposes and can be altered if they are not suitable. But this is where the most difficult dilemma of all occurs: can one make rational statements about the foundations of ethics and the choice between competing ends?

The moral dilemma

One leading philosopher, Alasdair MacIntyre, has argued at length (1980, 1981, 1988, 1990) that one cannot, in fact, make rational comments on the premises of moral systems: one must either accept or reject them. Commenting (in *After Virtue*) on two major competing systems, that of Rawls (1972) and that of Nozik (1974), he writes:

> Why should I accept Nozik's premises? He furnishes me with no reasons, but with a promissory note. Why should I accept Rawls's premises? They are, so he argues, those that would be accepted by hypothetical rational beings whose ignorance of their position in any social hierarchy enables them to plan a type of social order in which the liberty of each is maximised, in which inequalities are tolerated only insofar as they have the effect of improving the lot of the least well-off, and in which the good of liberty has the priority over that of equality.
>
> But why should I in my actual social conditions choose to accept what those hypothetical rational beings would choose, rather than for example Nozick's premises about natural rights? And why should I accept what Rawls says about the priority of liberty over equality?
>
> (MacIntyre, 1980: 22)

Is, then, any system as good as any other? It depends, MacIntyre argues, on your perspective. In a later study, *Whose Justice? Which Rationality?* (1988: 5–6), MacIntyre observes that 'we inhabit a culture in which an inability to arrive at agreed, rationally justifiable conclusions on the nature of justice and practical rationality coexists with appeals by contending social groups to sets of rival and conflicting convictions unsupported by rational justification.' Neither academic philosophy nor any other discipline has been able to supply ordinary citizens with ways of reaching conviction on matters of rational justification. Disputed questions, such as those concerning the nature and purpose of universities, are treated in the public realm not as matters for rational enquiry, but rather as occasions for assertion and counter-assertion.

Through a magisterial study of Plato, Aristotle, Augustine, Aquinas and Hume, and many individuals falling under their influences, MacIntyre explores the conception of *rational enquiry as embodied in a tradition*, a notion to which the Enlightenment search for universal rationality has made us, he argues, for the most part blind. A tradition in this sense is more than a coherent movement of thought. 'It is such a movement in the course of which those engaging in the movement become aware of it and of its direction and in self-aware fashion attempt to engage in its debates and to carry its enquiries forward'(MacIntyre, 1988: 326).

He demonstrates how the prevailing modern culture of liberalism has become transformed into a tradition – to the extent that those in its thrall do not realize the underlying assumptions that they are making. Rawls, he notes, equates the human self with the liberal self in a way that 'is atypical of the liberal tradition only in its clarity of conception and statement' (p. 337).

So anxious is the liberal perspective to accommodate all points of view, to recognize the preferences of individuals, that debate on matters of principle can have no effective resolution. The institutionalization of liberalism involves the tallying and weighing of expressions of preference, with all that that entails in the surveying of public opinion, responding to consumer choice and counting votes.

Agreement regarding matters of academic curriculum, teaching method and so forth requires, in the liberal tradition, primarily political agreement about, or assent to, procedures that involve no articulation of fundamental principle, but rather an accumulation of judgements by persons deemed acceptable to those judged by rules and procedures that appear fair. The mark of a liberal system, MacIntyre (1988: 344) notes, is to refer its conflicts for their resolution not to debates about any universal theory of human good, but rather to the verdicts of its legal system. The lawyers, not the philosophers, he suggests, are the clergy of liberalism.

So steeped are we in the assumptions of liberalism that we fail to notice that the starting points of liberal theorizing are always liberal starting points; they are never neutral between conceptions of the human good. MacIntyre argues that liberal theory is best understood not so much as the attempt to find a rationality independent of tradition as the articulation of a historically developed and developing set of social institutions and forms that themselves constitute a tradition – a tradition traceable to Enlightenment optimism about discovering a form of universal rationality.

MacIntyre's position, powerfully supported by his studies of a variety of philosophical perspectives, is that 'there is no other way to engage in the formulation, elaboration, rational justification, and criticism of accounts of practical rationality and justice except from within one particular tradition in conversation, cooperation, and conflict with those who inhabit the same tradition' (1988: 350). Each tradition develops rational justification for its central theses in its own terms; but there is no culturally independent set of standards to which the issues between contending traditions can be decided. Relativism, which denies that rational choice between rival traditions is possible, and perspectivism, which questions the possibility of making truth-claims from *within* any one tradition, are seen as the negative counterpart of the Enlightenment, 'its inverted mirror image'(p. 353). To be outside all traditions is to cut oneself off from serious enquiry: 'it is to be in a state of intellectual and moral destitution, a condition from which it is impossible to issue the relativist challenge' (p. 367).

We can perhaps realize how deeply we experience the tradition of liberalism when we realize how seriously we would regard putting liberalism itself in question. The intolerance of others, expressed, for example, in the one-time exclusion of Catholics and Jews from university posts, was replaced by a convention of appointing university teachers without considering their beliefs and allegiances, an appeal to conceptions of scholarly competence independent of standpoint. Similarly, teachers were expected to present what they taught in the classroom *as if* there were standards of rationality which all could and should accept.

MacIntyre (1988: 400) argues that these procedures did least harm to teaching and research into the natural sciences, where radical dissent (such as that of astrologers and phrenologists) could be readily extruded. Most harm, he suggests, was done to the humanities, in which the loss of contexts provided by traditions of enquiry has increasingly deprived those teaching of standards in the light of which some texts might be deemed more important than others.

What MacIntyre's analysis offers is not the end of a debate, but rather a point at which one can begin.

In addressing some of the specific problems of universities, in his later book *Three Rival Versions of Moral Enquiry* (1990), he notes 'the apparently ineliminable continuing divisions and conflicts within *all* humanistic enquiry. . . . In psychology, psychoanalysts, Skinnerian behaviourists, and cognitive theorists are as far from resolving their differences as ever. In political enquiry Straussians, Neo-Marxists, and anti-ideological empiricists are at least as deeply antagonistic. In literary theory and history deconstructionists, historicists, heirs of I. A. Richards and readers and misreaders of Harold Bloom similarly contend' (p. 6).

What is noteworthy is that the mutually incompatible doctrines that define the standpoints of major disciplines are accompanied by very high levels of skill in handling narrow questions of limited detail. Shared standards of argument in public debate render all debate inconclusive, yet we still behave as if the university did constitute a single, tolerably unified intellectual community.

MacIntyre's book is made up of the Gifford lectures delivered at the University of Edinburgh in 1988. He shows a becoming sensitivity to the possible irony of addressing lectures elaborating for a diverse audience his views on the need to locate philosophical views within a tradition. 'The most that one can hope for is to render our disagreements more constructive.' Yet he produces a powerful statement of the need for universities to be the very places where questions about what they are for are seriously addressed:

The beginning of any worthwhile answer to such questions, posed by some external critic, as 'What are universities for?' or 'What peculiar goods do universities serve?' should be, 'They are, when they are true to their own vocation, institutions in which questions of the form "What are x's for?" and "What peculiar goods do y's serve?" are formulated and answered in the best rationally defensible way.' That is to say, when it is demanded of a university community that it justify itself by specifying what its peculiar and essential function is, that function which, were it not to exist, no other institution could discharge, the response of that community ought to be that universities are places where conceptions of and standards of rational justification are elaborated, put to work in the detailed practices of enquiry, and themselves rationally evaluated, so that only from the university can the wider society learn how to conduct its own debates, practical or theoretical, in a rationally defensible way. But that claim itself can be plausibly and justifiably advanced only when and insofar as the university is a place where rival and antagonistic views of rational justification, such as those of genealogists and Thomists, are afforded the opportunity both to develop their own enquiries, in practice and in the articulation of the theory of that practice, and to conduct their intellectual and moral warfare. It is precisely because universities have not been such places and have in fact organised enquiry through institutions and genres well designed to prevent them and to protect them from being such places that the official responses of both the appointed leaders and the working members of university communities to their recent external critics have been so lamentable.

(MacIntyre, 1990: 222)

MacIntyre sees the university as 'a place of constrained disagreement' in which a central responsibility would be to initiate students into conflict.

The approach developed in the present book is to develop an argument within a tradition, and to delineate it primarily by sketching the resistances and preferences to which it gives rise. For this reason, and to sharpen focus on the position as much as possible, positions which deviate from it are called 'heresies' – a heresy being an exaggeration of 'the truth' in one direction or another.

A moral position

The moral position illustrated in the chapters which follow will seem crass when stated in bald, general terms: its value is in constituting a kind of 'situation ethics' which takes its life in concrete and specific contexts. Its roots are in Christian tradition, filtered through Enlightenment rationalism and existentialist criticism of rationalism; it is, in this sense, Christian-compatible (to use a phrase of Roy Niblett) rather than explicitly Christian. I describe it with the phrase liberal humanism, partly to distinguish it from the individualistic liberalism rightly criticized by MacIntyre, and also to signify that it is not an explicitly theological position, although I myself am a liberal Anglican (i.e. not high church or evangelical). I warn my readers of my adherence to this tradition, just as I warn the undergraduates to whom I teach modern literature and drama and sociology within the humanities programme at Imperial College. (If they are fully aware of my position, they can probe the source of my likes and dislikes, and be in a position to offer criticisms from their own cultural perspectives – which many, in fact, do – if they are so minded. Without this disclaimer, I might try to teach 'objectively' and, in consequence, lifelessly.)

The nourishment of persons

My central thesis is that without a view about the nourishment of persons, debate about the aims and purposes of universities is largely meaningless. Indeed, my assertion is that students should be the primary focus of concern for people in universities – who they are, and who their teachers and the students themselves hope they will become. It is wise to be overt about these matters; if one is not overt, then it is all too easy to be covert, and to import into university life, knowingly or unknowingly, ideas that students might resist if they knew them for what they were.

For sake of argument, I identify four aspects of the idea of a person that are fundamental:

Intellectual

Social   Personal

Practical

The social–personal axis reflects the issues of whether the individual's identity is primarily an aggregation of social roles (as much 'role theory' (see Banton, 1965) would apparently maintain) or if it is rather *sui generis* defined (as Sartre, 1965, for example would argue) by the choices each individual freely makes. Tiryakian (1962) describes these positions as, respectively, 'sociologism' and 'existentialism'.

The polarity is not, of course, a sharp one. Goffman, for example, in numerous studies (e.g. Goffman, 1963, 1969, 1972) has demonstrated how individuals deliberately and systematically manipulate roles in conscious modes of self-definition, albeit using, as it were, a vocabulary of role definitions which is socially constructed. More recently, Giddens (1991) discusses in detail what he calls the 'reflexive project of the self' – the process whereby self-identity is constituted by the reflexive ordering of self-narratives. Similarly, Grant (1994) reminds us that the concept of a person derives from the Greek word for face (Greek *prosopon*; Latin *persona*). Persons, in short, have much freedom of choice in determining their particular personalities, and in presenting themselves to others. For this very reason, questions regarding the nature of persons are at the centre of concern in many disciplines, e.g. literature and drama, philosophy, psychology, psychiatry, social anthropology, sociology, as well as those concerned with, for example,

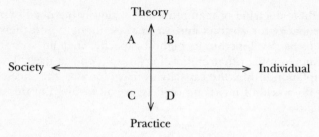

Figure 2.1 Institutional correlatives of the social personal, intellectual and practical dimensions of the person.

the effects of chemicals and other stimuli on mood and personality: biochemistry, biology, biophysics, chemistry and those branches of electrical and electronic engineering concerned with cognitive science.

In practice, we experience the dimensions of personality shown above as part of a totality: *who* we are depends upon how we balance the four concerns. What holds them together? For those of a theological frame of mind, I would suggest the spiritual; for those of a more secular temperament, I would suggest commitment.

Universities, having become the primary custodians of the rites of passage of modern society for many young people, can be seen as places where the nature of an individual's commitment is nourished, developed and celebrated. By accident or design, they institutionalize and embody notions of what it means to be a person; and, assuming that design is to be preferred to accident, I propose that the institutional correlatives of the above dimensions of the person are as shown in Figure 2.1.

The respect for persons involved in the liberal humanist perspective seeks for each individual a *balance* between these four preoccupations; and because we spend most of our lives in collaboration with one another through social institutions, it seeks a similar balance in institutional arrangements within the limits of what is possible – balance, that is, not only between the disposition of institutions in society, but *within* each type of institution so that no individual is reduced by his or her membership of that institution.

Although the notion of a person is a complex and contested one, as MacIntyre (1990), for example, demonstrates at length, I will be brief. (To do otherwise would require another book – one which I am not qualified to write.) A few comments on the axes of Figure 2.1 will indicate the broad position: details are filled out in each of the ensuing chapters.

Theory (ideas)
In many ways, the distinguishing marks of being human are those concerned with the mind: the organizing power of thought as revealed variously in works of art, scientific theories, political programmes and so forth. Hence the name *Homo sapiens.*

Any credible doctrine of man must take seriously the need of individuals for their capacity for abstract and/or analytic thought and their aesthetic sensibility to be developed to its highest capacity. Such an aspiration is not only a means to some other end; rather, it is an end in itself. The element of contemplation in life, the capacity we have for awe, the sheer delight of exploring the world of ideas and objects, are all involved in this dimension of personality.

Practice

Obviously, although we do not live by bread alone, we do live by bread. 'Practice' refers to everything concerned with the apparatus of living; by implication, because emotion is usually an expression of frustration when some such basic need is not satisfied, 'practice' also refers to the feelings which are organized or controlled through mind.

Competence in practice is usually seen as the means to an end; but our satisfaction and sense of fulfilment in doing, in the sheer mastery of technique, can also be seen in our use of the term *Homo faber*. It has been a mischief peculiar perhaps to English culture that *Homo sapiens* has been more esteemed over the past century than *Homo faber*.

The theory–practice axis is reminiscent of Freud's model of the super-ego, ego, and id. In more complex and subtle ways, it echoes theological concepts of the transcendent and the mundane. The society–individual axis, likewise, does not claim to be original: the dichotomy it represents, for example, is, as noted above, the substance of Tiryakian's *Sociologism and Existentialism* (1962).

Society

In an important sense, persons are aggregations of social roles; they cannot be described as definable entities except through language which locates the person as father, son, wife, daughter, factory-worker, citizen etc. Becoming acquainted with the requirements of social roles of various degrees of complexity is a major part of individual learning and is often the *raison d'être* of much education.

In contrast to the purely liberal position, a liberal *humanist* doctrine of man sees the development of the individual's social sense as fundamental. At one level, there is the business of enlarging and deepening our sense of involvement one with another. If the notion of moral progress means anything (see Ginsberg, 1961: Chapter 1), it must involve the progressive enlarging of the domain of our social concern: from family, to town, to country, to continent; indeed, the ecology movement rightly extends the area of moral concern to the well-being of generations as yet unborn. In short, we are enriched as people to the extent that we perceive and act upon our interdependencies.

Once again, the issue is as much one of affect as of social action. Part of the fascination of life is to contemplate the immense variety of social forms. Indeed, the single greatest consumer of people's leisure-time in the United

Kingdom is television-watching. Much of what is watched is dramatic fiction, which in turn relies absolutely on our views about the range of acceptable alternative behaviours.

Individual

If we treat persons as a sort of fluid that flows, or is poured, into a set of predefined social roles, we deny the fundamental element (upon which most existentialist writers insist) of a person's capacity for choice. Individuality, even eccentricity, is fundamental, even if most of us most of the time conform to social expectations. Our sense of what it is to be a person is constantly nourished by those who make unusual statements (in writing, music, paint, stone, by climbing improbable peaks, sailing alone around the world and so forth).

It is the mark of totalitarianism of all kinds that it treats individuals not as ends but as means – to the glory of the state or the power of dictators. A constantly refreshed sensitivity to what is unique in other people is another element of a liberal humanist doctrine of man.

My assertion is that a society which, by accident or by design, limits the opportunities of persons in any of the dimensions signified by these axes is at fault. 'The good life', in this perspective, is one in which persons are intellectually alert (stimulated by theories and ideas), with needs adequately provided for by the apparatus of social life (practice), responsive to and actively involved with the greatest possible range of institutions through which their society takes its life (society), yet able to exercise sufficient choice to define themselves as individuals.

Learning is the process by which persons establish their identity and commitment (intellectual, physical, social) within the matrix established by these axes; education is the social process by which this learning is given shape and direction. Education, as suggested in Chapter 1, implies organization, purpose, institutions. In every aspect of higher education (curriculum, teaching methods, research, collegial organization), choices have to be made of what can and should be done; specialization of function is an operational necessity. But the thesis of this book is that if education, in any institutional form, neglects any one of the needs of persons indicated above, it violates the tenets of liberal humanism.

Individuals may wish to become specialists in a particular area; however, educating institutions represent an act of collective will. While they and their members undoubtedly need to specialize for reasons of technical efficiency, the liberal humanist position here sketched seeks deliberate, systematic fidelity to the concept of a person to be expressed in institutional arrangements. If educational practice (in curriculum, teaching methods, research or college organization) drifts off into any one of the quadrants (A, B, C, D in Figure 2.1) to the neglect of the other issues involved in the concern for persons, some form of 'heresy' is in danger of being perpetrated. The chapters which follow illustrate this notion.

3

Curriculum

There have been many attempts to produce a systematic approach to the analysis of the curriculum; of these, those by Hirst (1974) and Phenix (1964) are well known, and those by Squires (1987, 1990) perhaps the most fruitful for the study of higher education.

For example, Squires (1990: Chapter 2) analyses the curriculum as knowledge in terms of object (physical, chemical, biological, human and artistic), stance (being, doing, knowing) and mode (philosophical, reflexive, normal) to produce a model that helps one to navigate one's way through some of the apparent difficulties in describing curricula in higher education. His concept of stance illustrates how the work of people apparently concerned with similar data, such as physicists, biologists, engineers and doctors, is not necessarily best distinguished by being pure rather than applied, or theoretical rather than practical, but can usefully be distinguished in terms of stance or intention or angle. Within these approaches, practitioners may be further distinguished by the mode of their working, whether this be normal (in Kuhn's (1962) sense of proceeding along and within lines that have become established as orthodox for the moment), reflexive (in the sense of constantly challenging assumptions) or philosophical (in which 'second-order questions' or 'meta-theories' are systematically examined in a sustained way). The differences are gradations, rather than mutually exclusive distinctions; but they help one to see that philosophy, for example, can be a mode of thinking in any discipline or a discipline in its own right.

Squires's model makes it possible to conceive of academic work in terms of 'disciplinary spaces' which readily become institutionalized in terms of the types of academic territory so lucidly described by Becher (1989). Squires's analysis leads to a picture of three types of culture, professional, academic and general, which, when located at the corners of a triangle, define the space within which any specific activities may be located.

Many of the most interesting and important questions about the design of curricula in higher education can also be located in the axes of Figure 2.1. Indeed, I would argue that if one's wish is (as it is the intention of this book) to evaluate what *could* be done against a perception of persons that leads to what *should* be done, the position is particularly fruitful.

A theory of knowledge is necessarily implied by the organizing ideas and concepts of disciplines. The personal philosophy of life of the individual can hardly help but be influenced by encounter with new ideas and information. Because curricula represent control of learning, they necessarily involve society in that those who devise curricula must be responsive (either by direct market forces or by more bureaucratic forms of accountability) to some other social agencies: the massive apparatus of accreditation, validation, evaluation and assessment is abundant witness to this. Finally, curricula relate to practice, if not by design, then by accident; even studies seemingly unrelated to the necessities of daily life (history, literature, philosophy etc.) impart personal and professional, transferable skills (such as those of careful reading, precise writing, the capacity to sift large quantities of information) which are fundamental in many forms of administration.

Each of the four factors is important on its own, but it is above all the attempt to maintain a reasonable *balance* between them for any individual person that makes education liberal. 'Heresies' which result from over-absorption with any one element are identified in this chapter.

Issues

In most academic disciplines, 'theory' constitutes a complex of ideas, internally consistent and rich in interconnections with other areas of enquiry, which gives perspective and order to a field of enquiry. As I have suggested elsewhere (Goodlad and Pippard, 1982; Goodlad, 1988), it is very often theory that distinguishes higher learning in its institutionalized forms from similar learning as undertaken by individuals. Compare, for example, a radio 'ham' with an electrical engineer, an antiquary with a historian, a naturalist with a botanist, a journalist with a political scientist. In each of the pairs, the first person listed accumulates ideas and information without the peer-pressure which an academic person experiences to fit him or her into complex intellectual frameworks.

There is no reason at all why people should not accumulate whatever information they desire. However, the collective will implied by educating institutions indicates the need for some principle of selection, some method of ordering perception. It is theory that distinguishes academic studies from their culturally primary forms: cooking/nutrition, construction/engineering, worship/theology, literature/literary criticism, politics/political science, musical performance/musicology. The primary form is just as useful and desirable as (often, in fact, more useful and desirable in some ways than) its theoretical correlate.

In higher education, institutional coherence often derives from a certain concentration of effort. Universities, for example, have concentrated on explanation, classification, analysis; other types of institution develop the primary cultural form directly (e.g. restaurants, factories, churches, theatres, parliament, orchestras) or as direct instruction for the exigencies of practice (e.g. hotel schools, training schools and technical colleges, theological seminaries, drama schools, political parties, conservatoires). For depth of understanding in any field of learning, however, it may well be necessary for a student of nutrition both to study biochemistry and to work in a kitchen, for an engineer both to study the strength of materials and economics and to work in a factory, for a theology student both to study biblical criticism and social doctrine and to work in a secular agency (whether or not directly concerned with social welfare or sponsored by a church), for a student of literature both to study literary criticism and to work in a publishing house or theatre, for a political science student both to study political theory and to work as a research assistant to a member of parliament or local councillor, for a music student both to study musicology and to play an instrument.

The emphasis on practice can not only, perhaps, prevent academic theory drifting off into meaninglessness or crankiness; in college curricula it may be a psychological necessity for students. Practice alone is, of course, not enough; without some coordinating theory, some inter-connectedness of ideas, purely practical subjects can ossify or degenerate into a congeries of rules of thumb and obsession with technique. Practice without theory can become basely conservative; theory without practice can become arcane, unintelligible or simply trivial. The obvious practical implication of these remarks is that just as it may be desirable for students in institutions which emphasize theory (e.g. universities) to be exposed to practice, so it may be desirable for students in institutions which emphasize practice (trade or vocational schools) to be exposed to theory.

With structural unemployment becoming, it seems, a growing menace in many societies, it is no kindness to individuals at any level of education to leave them without skills with which to earn a living. But this does not imply transforming education into skills training; rather, it may involve the systematic analysis of marketable skills which an individual acquires while pursuing studies which are not specifically related to work. Counselling and career guidance may be necessary to prevent students feeling that they have to neglect the transcendent in pursuit of the mundane.

On the society–individual axis, the principal issue is that of autonomy and accountability. Individual persons need time and space in which to work out their personal philosophies of life. How, when, where is this to be provided? It is not enough for educating institutions to say that this is someone else's business (churches, political parties, parents); some sort of facilitating activity is required in the curriculum, offering students the opportunity (which not all, of course, may wish to take) to reflect on matters of ultimate concern. (Later in this chapter I offer some suggestions about how this may be done.) What makes life complicated is that the need or desire for opportunities for reflection occurs at different ages for different individuals, as William Perry (1970, 1981), for example, has shown.

The emphasis on society in the discussion of curricula recalls that academic disciplines are institutional phenomena, with all the apparatus of learned societies, peer assessment, journals and so forth. Academic knowledge is

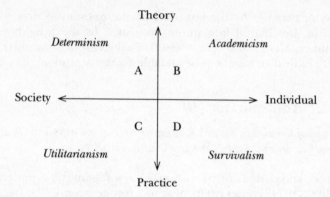

Figure 3.1 The heresies of curriculum.

consensus knowledge. In the formation of knowledge (a point to be discussed in Chapter 5), the freedom of individual scholars to follow ideas wherever they may lead has preserved the individual *vis-à-vis* society. In the dissemination of knowledge through curricula, what nowadays preserves the freedom of the individual educating institutions or of individual teachers and students within them? Again, some balance of interests is desirable.

Heresies

With the division of labour in society, and the consequent specialization of interests, there is a constant tendency for 'heresies' to spring up in the prescription of curricula. Each of the four listed here represents an attempt, in many ways laudable, to stress the importance of one or other aspect of curriculum – but does so at the expense of the others. The letters after the heresies represent the quadrant of Figure 3.1 into which the 'heresy' has drifted.

Heresy 1: Determinism (A)

Belief in the exclusively social genesis of knowledge and overstatement of the (often undeniable) class interest in knowledge.

The fruitful (Marxist) notion that the superstructure of ideas (theory) is heavily dependent upon the activity of interest groups becomes heretical whenever it is claimed that the curriculum is, could or should be entirely formed by social process. To deny the possibility or opportunity of individuals creating unique syntheses of ideas in their studies is fundamentally anti-humanist.

Dr Johnson's tart comment, 'We *know* our will is free, and *there's* an end on't', may or may not be the last word on the question of free will versus determinism. But liberal humanism, nourished by the insights of Sartre, Camus, Buber, Marcel and others, asserts (as against determinists) that it is possible for individual insight to be valuable above the wisdom of committees.

Heresy 2: Academicism (B)

Reification of knowledge, found whenever disciplines are defined as though they were somehow independent of the people who created them.

The phrase 'knowledge for its own sake' is sometimes a symptom of this heresy. Hirst (1974) comes pretty near to a restatement of Platonic idealism in his thesis about 'forms' and 'fields' of knowledge, although he denies commitment to any such position. Certainly, with mathematics, there is a certain givenness about the inner logic of the discipline which is compelling; but with every other type of knowledge, analyses fall back upon conventions of description, concentrations of interest, which while (in their more highly developed forms) relatively inexplicable to those not versed in the disciplines, are ultimately traceable to individual intellectual concerns. In many ways, academicism is antithetical to determinism, but only as a competitor – urging the apparent givenness and immovability of subject matter.

Academicism is placed in segment B because it indicates a detachment of the individual (academic or student) from any realistic perception of what is either socially desirable or practically meaningful. Thus, a very common symptom of academicism is the assertion that, if students are to be properly educated, it is necessary to 'cover the ground' (whatever that may mean). The baleful consequence can be that syllabuses can be cluttered with so many facts that students have neither the time nor the opportunity to reflect on the meaning the subject might have for them personally or for society more widely. Ironically, academicism seems to flourish as vigorously in vocational subjects, such as engineering and medicine, as in non-vocational ones, such as history.

Heresy 3: Utilitarianism (C)

The adaptationist tendency to see learning always as a means to some social end, concerned with 'practice', never as a source of personal enlightenment, revelation or satisfaction to the individual.

The utilitarian heresy is in constant danger of appearing whenever manpower-planning goals come to dominate educational thinking. It appears in quadrant C because it is often the result of well-meaning committee work which tidies out of existence the slow, muddied, baroque quality of learning, which may involve 'playing with ideas' or the simple accumulation of information for delight. If the desire for social relevance in studies is kept in balance with other factors, it can be a considerable source of wisdom; total absorption with quadrant C is stultifying. Falling into this heresy (as is explained further below) is some recent writing in the United Kingdom about National Vocational Qualifications (NVQs).

Heresy 4: Survivalism (D)

The over-emphasis on education as supplying job skills.

Survivalism is often the heresy which permits utilitarianism to flourish: it is the obsession of individuals with seeking in education primarily readily cashable skills for earning a living. The danger of survivalism, as with utilitarianism, on which it feeds, is that of defining skills in terms of today's problems rather than tomorrow's possibilities.

The old cliché that we work to live rather than live to work points out the ultimate futility of activity (and learning leading towards it) which is overly absorbed with survival. Why, to use Samuel Beckett's phrase, give birth astride a grave? It may be pretty difficult to keep in mind on a practical course of training the object of extending people's horizons: but without such concern, education or training is selling people short.

Preferences

This section of the chapter does not seek to prescribe a formula for curriculum design; rather it mentions some preferences of 'good practice'. It cannot be emphasized too strongly that these remarks are about the curriculum in institutions specifically devoted to education. There are obviously institutional contexts in which learning (even teaching as such) takes place where it may be less necessary to seek such balance: research institutes (perhaps concerned with pure theory), factories etc. The decision we face is one concerning institutional priorities: what should be done, when, where, why and how by particular *sorts* of institution. The remarks that follow concern universities as one type of specialized institution.

Reflexivity

So easy is it to drift into one or other form of heresy, that the first desideratum is of a reflective component in any course of study, an opportunity to be self-conscious and critically aware of *why* any particular component of the syllabus is there or what it is that one is seeking to achieve.

This reflection may, *inter alia*, involve viewing the apparent certainties of one discipline from the perspective of some other (commentating) discipline in which they may appear as less than certain. The 'theory' involved in higher education could be deemed its distinguishing feature. Teachers in higher education may not know more than (they may even know less than) the individual practitioner: the radio 'ham' may have more raw information than the electrical engineer, the antiquary more specific facts than the historian, and so on. There is no limit to the amount of information that could be sought, but facts alone are not the stuff of education. As Whitehead (1932: 1) crisply observed, 'A merely well-informed man is the most useless bore on God's earth.'

I have argued elsewhere (Goodlad, 1976) that teachers in higher education exhibit the defining characteristic of possessing 'authoritative uncertainty' when they know, on the basis of highly organized study, what it is worth trying to find out and why. They have, in short, a principle of selection. Their uncertainty is not the uncertainty of sheer ignorance, but the uncertainty of deep learning. To be able to decide what is the next thing worth studying, and to have the inner conviction about potentially fruitful ways of proceeding, is commonly regarded as the defining characteristic of students worthy of upper-second or first class honours. For the student to come some way towards this experience of 'authoritative uncertainty' is a consummation devoutly to be wished: it is, perhaps, a defence against determinism and academicism. It is an intellectual approach common to many endeavours; it is also a highly transportable personal and professional skill.

One method of achieving the critical, self-conscious 'cultural migration' from the orbit of one's main discipline is to view it from the perspective of another, from which the 'certainties' may look less certain. For this purpose (see Goodlad and Pippard, 1982: 76) physics could be inspected from the perspective of philosophy, literature from anthropology, engineering from economics, philosophy from sociology, anthropology from history etc. The 'disturbing' perspective will vary from discipline to discipline: some disciplines even provide their own disturbing perspectives, such as the phenomenon of sociologies of sociology (Gouldner, 1971; Friedrichs, 1972). What is required in each case, however, is the attempt to stimulate in students an awareness of the strengths and weaknesses of specific intellectual positions, and the capacity to relate specific technical concerns to issues of wider social, political, economic and philosophical concern. So-called 'liberal studies' in engineering degrees have frequently had this objective. A brief case study of the provision of humanities courses at Imperial College will illustrate this point.

The humanities at Imperial College
The present provision of humanities options in the degree studies of students at Imperial College is the result of initiatives taken in the 1970s.

The narrowness of British higher education received significant public attention in the 1960s, through the Robbins Committee (1963), the Dainton Committee (1968) and the Swann Committee (1968). At Imperial College, the student union also expressed itself strongly in favour of 'diversification' of studies. Accordingly, the then Pro-rector, Sir Willis Jackson, commissioned two studies to ascertain the extent of demand. The first, a study of 'the demand for non-technical studies at Imperial College' (Goodlad *et al.*, 1970) asked all undergraduates whether or not they would wish to take non-technical studies for credit, and if 'yes' which subject they would most favour. Over 50 per cent of students responded and, of these, over 90 per cent (i.e. 45 per cent of all students) were strongly in favour of such studies becoming part of the degree. The subsequent pattern of provision and take-up has reflected very closely the demand discovered by this study.

The second study, carried out by Professor Goodger (Goodger and Tilley, 1970), asked alumni what, with hindsight, they would like to have been able to study. Again, a strong pattern of demand for humanities and social sciences emerged.

Simultaneously, the Schools Council (1970) had discovered that 36 per cent of those taking only science A levels would have liked to study a mixture of science and arts. (Since then, many young people have actually taken mixtures of science and arts A levels: for example, 23,615 in 1988 (UCCA, 1989: Table D6). These include some of the brightest young people: of those with four A-level passes, 4,538 combined science and social science, and 3,603 combined science and arts.)

In the light of this information, Professor David Raphael was appointed in 1973 as the first Academic Director of Associated Studies. Individual humanities teachers who had been appointed to serve the needs of specific (engineering) departments were subsequently grouped into the Humanities Department (which taught humanities and languages) and (what later became) the Department of Social and Economic Studies (which taught economics and industrial sociology). The Humanities Department later became the Humanities Programme, with the history of science, technology and medicine group being established as a quasi-department. The Department of Social and Economic Studies became the nucleus of the present Management School. The main subject departments of the college are able to offer to their students combinations of subjects offered by these providers.

Recent years have seen a steady growth in student demand for courses offered by the Humanities Programme:

1987–8	1988–9	1989–90	1990–1	1991–2	1992–3
1,201	1,453	1,781	1,861	1,849	2,315

The growth between 1987–8 and 1992–3 has been 93 per cent. Stimulated by the increasing number of degree courses with a year abroad, and perhaps by an extension of the college's teaching day, there was a growth even between 1991–2 and 1992–3 of 25 per cent.

The ends

The object of the Humanities Programme is to offer to all students who desire it the opportunity to consider some of the central moral, political and social issues of contemporary society.

The means
Students are exposed to the styles of thinking that characterize selected disciplines and fields of the humanities – the disciplines being modes of discourse that generate their own subject matter, the fields being clusters of conceptual problems associated with specific practical activities.

Language courses not only impart skills but also examine some of the ideas and institutions of the various countries. Where the immediate focus is a technical skill, such as the presentation of technical information, questions that lead into wider issues are raised regarding what is being communicated to whom for what purpose. Present provision of courses falls into four clusters.

1 Courses dealing directly with the fundamental nature of science and technology:
    philosophy of science;
    history of science;
    history of technology.
2 Courses dealing with theoretical issues of intellectual significance to all people:
    philosophy;
    modern European history;
    modern literature & drama;
    communication of scientific ideas: sociology.
3 Courses developing practical skills against a theoretical background:
    communication of scientific ideas: practical;
    presentation of technical information.
4 Language courses preparing students to expose themselves directly to the full complexity of other countries and cultures (in some cases by a year of study abroad):
    French;
    German;
    Italian;
    Japanese;
    Russian;
    Spanish.

The approach
The humanities courses do not attempt to inculcate a common culture: they are not 'great books' courses, nor are they survey courses, nor are they concerned with 'gentlemanly cultivation'. Rather, they emphasize the intellectual processes that highlight specific artifacts, events, or ideas as ones that merit attention.

Although we want our students to be well-informed, the emphasis in the courses is on identifying key issues in complex situations, on evaluating arguments in which judgement rather than numerical analysis has to be applied; in short, on disciplined thought rather than primarily on specific facts. For this reason, all courses involve significant amounts of coursework in the form of essay-writing.

The language courses aim to bring students who will be spending a year abroad to the level at which they can read, understand and speak the language so as to work effectively alongside students native to the country to be visited.

The time involved

For students studying languages, three hours of instruction per week plus three hours of private study for two terms is the norm; that is, 120 hours in the academic year (or 10 per cent of a 1,200 hour – 30 weeks × 40 hours – working year). For students entering with a Grade B at GCSE, two years of study is necessary to bring them to the level at which to study abroad. Humanities courses are designed to occupy similar amounts of time, i.e. 120–150 hours in the academic year.

The college committee responsible for the policy governing these activities, the Humanities Committee, believes that all students should have the opportunity (though without compulsion) to devote at least 10 per cent of their total study time to the humanities or languages, and receive academic credit in due proportion. We are, at present, some way from achieving this.

What liberal studies should not try to do

Quite apart from the danger of sliding into heresies, the provision of humanities for students of technical professional studies must avoid a number of other snares and pitfalls. Some of these have been lucidly outlined by Moulakis (1993), who describes the thinking behind the founding of a new and innovative programme of humanities for engineers at the University of Colorado, Boulder, USA, in 1989.

As we have done at Imperial College, so has Moulakis at Boulder rejected the notion that 'liberal studies' is a residual category of disciplines that are not vocational, technical or scientific. Responding to the perceptions of American engineers themselves, and of engineering employers, that the education of engineers is too narrow, Moulakis describes additions to the curriculum whose object is to help students to become articulate in speech and writing and better able to exercise informed judgement.

Gentlemanly cultivation, the development of foppish social graces, would be wholly unacceptable where the ideal engineer is seen as 'a regular guy, a red-blooded American who stirs his coffee with his thumb'. Nor is familiarity with 'great books' commended: the approach pioneered at Chicago by Robert M. Hutchins ('The best education for the best is the best education for all'), or its quiz-programme imitation, E. D. Hirsch's *Cultural Literacy: What Every American Needs to Know* (1987), which reduces culture to a mass of inert pieces of information. Progressive education, too, gets short shrift from Moulakis: 'Behind "fundamental processes," "cognitional skills," and "critical thinking," taught by a teacher who has himself been taught nothing but "education," there is nothing.' The current American obsession with 'the canon' or core of books leading to quintessential liberal education is seen to miss the point of pedagogical efforts to help students towards maturity of judgement, rather than to be simply well-informed about civilization.

Having fired well-aimed shots at relativism (which implicitly denies the basis of its own validity), at Marxist cultural analysis (where it becomes impossible to discern what explains from what is being explained), at 'herstory' (the ruthlessly feminist approach to culture that risks obliterating one myth with another rather than cultivating a balanced perspective) and at the notion put around by Linus Pauling that science carries within itself its own morality, Moulakis identifies as the greatest enemy of liberal education the attempt to 'cover the ground'. This he calls 'the Sisyphian project of complete enumeration' which is 'but a prolongation of the widespread misconception that knowledge is primarily a matter of registering and filing away facts, as though facts were given and did not need to be established.'

Moulakis rightly observes that the bridge between technical and humanistic cultures will not be built by adding chapters to textbooks, or even by creating an interdisciplinary supertextbook; rather it is to be sought by giving engineers an opportunity to know what it means to know in the manner of a historian or of a physicist, that is to say to understand a particular mode of human enquiry and its terms of reference. Although one obviously cannot 'learn how to learn' without actually learning something, the object of liberal education, in Moulakis's view, should not be to create a modern version of the Renaissance polymath, but rather to encourage the ability to place, evaluate and appreciate whatever the graduate comes across – and to be equipped to take an effective part in the political process by being able to distinguish between politically necessary technical information and the structures of political responsibility.

Other approaches
Again, as I have argued elsewhere (Goodlad and Pippard, 1982; Goodlad, 1988), one useful form of the experience of uncertainty can be generated by the application of ideas to new conditions – for example, through project work where the student has the opportunity to make a personal synthesis of ideas. What is important is for the student to experience the excitement and delight of trying to make sense of data by constructing (or using) concepts or hypotheses, even if these turn out to be 'wrong' when viewed from the vantage point of wider information. This approach, more properly seen as a method of teaching rather than the substance of learning, is more fully explored below.

A variation on project work, particularly suited to research universities, is that of undergraduate research opportunities (see MacVicar and McGavern, 1984). Opportunities have been provided at the Massachusetts Institute of Technology since 1969, and at the Imperial College of Science, Technology and Medicine since 1981, to let students work alongside faculty and share some of the agony and ecstasy of the full range of their professional responsibilities. One significant advantage of undergraduate research opportunities

over traditional project work is that the students can join an on-going programme of work rather than involve the faculty in the (logistically complex)
task of finding chunks of doable work which would fit into a given curriculum time slot. The use of undergraduate research opportunities is further
explored below as one administrative and pedagogical procedure by which
a university can draw undergraduates into a collegial sharing of one of its
central purposes.

Problem-based study

A common theme in the student experience of humanities for science and
engineering students, of project work and of problem-based learning is the
satisfaction of studying something in depth. In the Humanities Programme
at Imperial College, this is achieved primarily through having students write
substantial essays on topics seen as significant within the framework of the
disciplines they are studying.

It may seem a paradox that they find depth in studies which represent
only about one-tenth of a given year's work. Surely one might expect the
depth to be experienced through the taking of a single-subject honours
degree? But this is to overlook the fact that single-subject honours degrees
often consist of a number of parallel courses interwoven in a very full
timetable.

That discipline-based study can result in incoherence at the level of student
experience is vividly illustrated by Schumacher (1994) in an account of the
restructuring of a social studies course at a former polytechnic. To re-create
the experience of students in following and trying to understand the original
sequence of lectures during the first year, Schumacher had a list of the
lectures typed up on cards. The title of each lecture, plus a brief synopsis,
was typed on to a separate card. The cards were stacked in chronological
order and then numbered – so that card 1 described the first lecture on the
morning of the first day of the academic year, card 2 the next lecture, and
so on throughout the 124 lectures given in the first year.

Schumacher's study showed that, at the level of students' experience, it
was difficult to detect any coherence at all. In an exercise which readers
might wish to emulate, Schumacher then invited small groups of students
to rearrange shuffled sets of cards into sequences determined only by their
own educational needs, as perceived by themselves. The results of this
exercise differed widely from the discipline-based programme. The students unanimously preferred a *thematic model*, centred on clusters of recognizable life-related experiences. In a similar exercise, the academic staff
themselves rearranged the cards in a way which reduced the disciplinary
emphasis in favour of recognizable themes. In short, the discipline-based
course construction that dominates many fields of (particularly professional)
study appeared to be inappropriate – certainly so for students in the first
year of a social studies course.

It is a similar perception that has led to the development of problem-based study, one of the potentially most fruitful ways of maintaining the balance between theory and practice, society and the individual in university work.

Very often project work is problem-based, but not all problem-based study is project work. For example, the Macmaster Medical School in Canada (Barrows and Tamblyn, 1980: Neufeld and Chong, 1984) arranged for students to learn medicine by confronting a graded series of problems of patient care. The procedure was adopted originally not only because it was clear that students quickly forgot what they heard in parallel theory-based lecture courses, but also because students who were going to have to practise as professionals, often isolated from the support of the medical school, needed to learn how to learn – so that they could cope with new situations and the massive yearly increase in knowledge of medicine mediated to them through floods of journal articles and the promotional literature of drug companies. Accordingly, students are not given lectures in the conventional sense. Rather, they are presented (through live interviews, simulations and other methods) with the sort of multidimensional problems encountered by physicians in practice; for example, chest pains which may have complex social and psychological, as well as physiological, causes. Students draw upon whatever resources of medical theory or of practical investigation that they think may help; but always they have to remain aware of the costs of what they undertake (the financial accountability in ordering more tests than are necessary, and the moral responsibility in ordering fewer).

As described by Barrows and Tamblyn (1980), the method involves the following six steps:

1 The problem is encountered first in the learning sequence, before any preparation or study has occurred.
2 The problem situation is presented to the student in the same way it would present in reality.
3 The student works with the problem in a manner that permits his ability to reason and apply knowledge to be challenged and evaluated, appropriate to his level of learning.
4 Needed areas of learning are identified in the process of work with the problem and used as a guide to individualized study.
5 The skills and knowledge acquired by this study are applied back to the problem, to evaluate the effectiveness of learning and to reinforce learning.
6 The learning that has occurred in work with the problem and in individualized study is summarized and integrated into the student's existing knowledge and skills.

By this method (which seems to be both efficient in producing graduates with few drop-outs and popular as a recruiting device for students), some of the more serious curriculum heresies may be avoided. Interestingly, the Macmaster Medical School also respects the interests and needs of the individual student by providing option courses in which students freed from the encounter with graded problems follow an interest wherever it may lead.

Problem-based medical education has been started in new medical schools in various parts of the world: for example, Newcastle in New South Wales, Maastricht in Holland and Beersheba in Israel. In the United Kingdom, the General Medical Council has determined that problem-based study should be adopted by all medical schools by the turn of the century (GMC, 1994). The basic technique is, however, applicable to other disciplines.

The case studies assembled by Boud (1985) show the very wide range of other professions to which problem-based study can contribute. For example, Smith (1985: Chapter 9) shows how in social work education a number of problem situations were chosen for study by the students that extended across life stage, social work setting and level of intervention. Implicit in the choice of problems was the view that social work is an ethical and political enterprise, that it has some features that distinguish it from other professions, and that it depends a great deal on the personal resources of the worker. Smith's chapter sets out with admirable clarity the objectives, modes of assessment and so forth of the programme and lists seven problems that were used as a focus of study:

1 A frail elderly couple unable to manage on their own.
2 Intergenerational conflict within a Lebanese family.
3 A 45-year-old woman with six children, on Supporting Parent Benefit, is brought to Credit Line on Warrant of Apprehension.
4 Premature birth of a first baby, who requires several months in an intensive care nursery.
5 Tenants of a Housing Commission estate concerned about lack of community facilities.
6 An Aboriginal father, backed by community groups, resists pressure to have his three children declared wards of the state.
7 A young man quadriplegic following a driving accident.

The Australian students presented with these authentic problems had a real incentive to learn, and came to see their tutor not as a purveyor of information, but rather as a resource and facilitator who aided their learning through guidance, questioning and challenging. Other examples are offered in the fields of economics, metallurgy, environmental health, management, architecture and agriculture.

In an admirable review of problem-based learning courses, Boud (1985: 15–16) notes some additional characteristics as follows: (a) an acknowledgement of the base of experience of learners; (b) an emphasis on students taking responsibility for their own learning; (c) their multidisciplinary or transdisciplinary nature; (d) the intertwining of theory and practice; (e) a focus on the process of knowledge acquisition rather than simply the products of such processes; (f) the changed role of staff from that of instructor to that of facilitator; (g) A change in the focus of assessment from staff assessment of the outcomes of student learning to greater self-assessment by students; (h) the explicit attention often given to communication and human relations skills even in highly technical areas.

There is a great deal still to be learned about problem-based study procedures, but the experiments noted above suggest that they bode well to unite the concerns of theory and practice, society and individual, that would steer clear of the worst heresies of curriculum.

Experiential learning

A superordinate category which embraces both project work and problem-based study is experiential learning – although an image of overlapping circles is perhaps more appropriate than that of enclosure. Experiential learning is interesting and important because, through an emphasis on making creative use of the learner's full range of experiences (not only in formal education, but also outside formal education), both content and contexts are open to negotiation; it celebrates the possibility that the learner may have as much to contribute to the negotiation of curriculum as the university teacher, although the learner's contribution is likely to be of a different, less formalized, nature. Experiential learning, perhaps more than other modes of learning, seeks to keep burning the flame of delight and attachment so vividly explored by Marjorie Reeves (1988).

The very process of institutionalization involved in organizing learning by the device of curriculum carries the danger of each type of heresy so far discussed. Experiential learning does not, by any means, uniquely offer salvation; it does, however, provide for the possibility of negotiation between teacher and taught, and may in this regard be more suited to adult or mature students than conventional types of curriculum.

The fundamental need for a curriculum comes from the need for measurement (the root of the word is the Latin *currus* – a light chariot – and the word 'course' associated with curriculum reminds one that a race of some sort is usually at issue). If measurement could be carried out of learning acquired other than under the direction, control and supervision of university teachers, considerable loosening of heresy-heavy rigidities could be contemplated.

In the United Kingdom, 'sandwich courses' involving periods of time spent in industry or other places of work have been in place for many years (see, for example, Smithers, 1976). There has also been a growth of interest in activities involving interwoven periods of work experience and academic study designed to develop personal and professional transferable skills – often of an entrepreneurial nature. Such work has been promoted by agencies such as the Education for Capability Unit of the Royal Society of Arts, the Enterprise in Higher Education (EHE) Initiative of the Department of Employment, the Partnership Awards Scheme initiated by the Council for Industry and Higher Education, and the Council for National Vocational Qualifications. Much of this activity is fuelled (sometimes misguidedly) by

Table 3.1 Requirements of CAEL techniques

Step	Application
Particular learning	Decide on general learning goals that are related to the degree objective
Identify learning	Set specific learning objectives that fit the goals and the learning site
Evaluate learning	Determine the appropriate criterion standard required for credit
Document learning	Maintain an integrated record as evidence of learning
Measure learning	Determine whether learning meets the criterion standard previously set
Transcribe learning	Record the credit or recognition of learning

the writings of Martin Wiener (1981) and Correlli Barnett (1986), even though their thesis (that English culture has been antipathetic to the industrial spirit) has been successfully challenged – for example, by Edgerton (1991).

In the United States of America, the Council for Adult and Experiential Learning (CAEL) has pioneered techniques for accrediting learning acquired outside formal educational settings, for example, through life and/ or work experience, through study-service or service-learning, etc. The emphasis of the techniques is rightly not simply on logging experience, but rather on assessing what has been *learned* from that experience. The basic requirements (see, for example, Willingham, 1977; Doyle and Chickering, 1982) are shown in Table 3.1.

The applications of the assessment of prior experiential learning (APL as it has come to be known) are many and various, as Norman Evans has shown (see Evans, 1981, 1983, 1984a, b, 1987, 1988). Indeed, the growth in the flow of literature about experiential learning over recent years has been remarkable: see, for example, the bibliography offered by Anderson (1985); case studies and analysis offered by Boydell (1976), Chickering (1977), Keeton *et al.* (1977), Brooks and Althof (1979), Moore (1981), Conrad and Hedin (1982a), Boot and Reynolds (1983), Boud *et al.* (1985), Weil and McGill (1989) and Further Education Unit (n.d.); advice on how experiential schemes can be organized in Davis *et al.* (1977), Duley (1978), ACTION (1979) and Stanton and Ali (1987); and studies of how learning derived from experience can be evaluated and assessed in ACTION (1978), Hendel and Enright (1978), Yelon and Duley (1978), Conrad and Hedin (1982b) and Duley (1982).

The retrospective analysis of knowledge and skills acquired in non-formal learning settings can permit *inter alia* freedom of movement between occupations, late entry into higher education (and/or into new jobs) without the individual having to go back to square one and credit-transfer between educating institutions. Experiential learning, if retrospectively analysed and accredited, is an obvious preference for the freedom of movement it offers. A word of caution is, however, necessary.

It is possible to try to go *too* far in documenting and measuring learning. A case in point is the growing movement in the United Kingdom for National Vocational Qualifications (NVQs) (see, for example, Bees and Swords, 1990; Field and Drysdale, 1991; Fletcher, 1991; Jessup, 1991). Starting with the laudable objectives of trying to tidy up the jungle of vocational qualifications and chart the learning people acquire 'on the job', with a view to permitting and encouraging people to seek formal recognition for what they have informally learned, the NVQ movement does not seem to be sure where to stop. The emphasis on outcomes of learning and on competent *performance* runs the danger of driving an otherwise worthwhile initiative into the heresy of utilitarianism. Knowledge as such is seen as a 'problem' (e.g. Fletcher, 1991: 55–6; Jessup, 1991: Chapter 18). Jessup, for example, writes:

> Coping with variation, as opposed to performing routine and procedur-alized functions, provides a primary distinction between low level and high level occupations in the NVQ framework. In particular, coping with variation which cannot be anticipated is characteristic of the most demanding jobs, at the forefront of development and innovation in a profession.
>
> Thus we need to assess in NVQs to cope with variation in practice which cannot be assessed through performance demonstrations. Within a competence-based model of qualifications there is no justification for assessing knowledge for its own sake but only for its contribution to competent performance.
>
> (Jessup, 1991: 122–3)

Without doubt there have to be agreed standards of competence in standardized and routine functions, though even with basic skills of craftsmanship and commerce there is an inherent danger of rigidity creeping in if everything is prescribed too tightly in advance. But should the same academic accountancy be applied to *all* fields of activity? In some areas linked with fast-moving research, such as information systems engineering (which encompasses computing science, computer science, electronic and electrical engineering), the field is changing so quickly that any definitive description of the occupation would be obsolete as soon as it were to be published. There would seem to be a strong case for activities in higher education for both academic staff and students to follow ideas wherever they may lead. This is not 'knowledge for its own sake' as much as knowledge for *our* sake – as stimulus to the imagination.

While an emphasis on practice is valuable for locating any theory that students may be learning, too rigid an obsession with academic accountancy may kill the very plant it seeks to nourish. A tide is creeping up around the feet of university people of which they should beware. Universities should, in my view, be very cautious about letting the fashion for vocational qualifications destroy the ebb and flow of ideas by which they live.

Independent study

The principle of systematic analysis of what has *been* learned rather than the prescription of what *has to be* learned can be an exceptionally fruitful approach for universities. It is the animating force behind schools of independent study, such as those at the University of Lancaster and the University of East London (formerly East London Polytechnic) (see Percy and Ramsden, 1980).

The growth of independent study at the University of East London, for example, has gone through a number of important stages, which are chronicled in detail by Robbins (1988). Based originally on an innovative two-year Diploma in Higher Education, the programme has held constant to one key principle: that each student's work should be determined primarily by what the student wanted to learn, rather than the student being stretched on a Procrustean bed of course requirements.

An early document quoted by Robbins (1988: 80) sets this out:

At the end of the programme the students should, without depending on external support, be able to:

1 formulate their own education problems, and propose their own solutions;
2 implement such solutions without imposed dependence upon the traditional;
3 monitor and subsequently readjust when necessary the progress and direction of their solutions;
4 judge the success or failure of their solutions and to engage in external dialogue on the validity of their judgements;
5 work in collaboration with others on the formulation of problems related to the needs of the community;
6 work with people and on projects not directly related to their own immediate expertise.

After completing the two-year DipHE, during which they bring their ideas to a focus, students are required to submit a detailed study plan somewhat like a 'research' proposal (quote marks are used because the proposals are often in the creative arts as well as in academic studies concerned with words and numbers). If the so-called Registration Board approves, the student completes a BA or BSc by a further year of honours-level study, based on the very detailed registration proposal.

The proposal put to the Registration Board: gives a personal statement showing in detail how the proposed work arises from the student's personal circumstances and interests, and how it will contribute to his or her personal and professional development; identifies the student's main final product (which may be a dissertation and/or an object or objects); lists the coursework and/or examinations that are to be taken (assigning, within a broad framework, the proportion of credit to be sought for each item); itemizes the resources of the university and/or outside agencies upon which the student intends to draw (enclosing any necessary permissions from relevant authorities); presents a full bibliography of proposed reading; and gives a timetable indicating when and how the work is to be carried out. This stringent requirement helps students to understand the principles of curriculum design and the need for an underlying structuring of ideas as well as specific items of information. In short, undergraduate students are able to shape the content of their studies as much as, often even more than, traditional postgraduate students.

During the period (in the late 1980s) when I was chief external examiner for the BA/BSc by independent study, there was a separate School for Independent Study; since then, independent study has become a mode of study available within the other schools of the university. Indeed, it is as a mode of study, rather than necessarily the animating principle of an entire degree course, that I guess the approach might commend itself to other universities. In Chapter 4, I sketch how this might be done.

Independent study has proved particularly attractive to mature and/or part-time students, who are a growing presence in higher education. My own observations of the outputs of degrees by independent study suggest that it is, indeed, most fruitful when students are, in Squires's phrase, information-rich and able and willing to seek and use analytic frameworks (the stuff of academic disciplines) that seek to relate particulars to organizing principles. Where this was not done well, there was a danger of students sinking in an interdisciplinary ooze; but the attempt by most students to 'make sense' of detail by reference to some system of thought probably taught them more about the strengths and weaknesses of academic disciplines than is learned by students on conventional courses, who can too easily be swept along on a tide without appreciating the forces that shape the current.

Although the animating ideas of the promoters of independent study are many and various, the practice is in harmony with the position being explored in this book. A preoccupation with the nourishment of persons as fundamental to good practice involves the university teacher in sharing with the learner his or her perception of the fundamental coordinating concepts of the discipline on which they are both engaged. Those types of independent study that set out to do just this are, therefore, an obvious preference. This matter is, however, as much one of method as it is of content. It is, therefore, to teaching methods that we now turn.

4

Teaching Methods

Issues

In one sense, teaching methods only become important in situations of constraint, where people are required to learn things which by natural inclination they would not learn or in which they need help and advice. Indeed, 'teaching' may in some instances interfere with learning by interrupting the rhythm and thrust of curiosity. How may one choose teaching methods that are the most supportive of, and least obstructive to, learners?

Theories of learning range from the highly structured behaviourism of B. F. Skinner (1968, 1971), through the 'Gestaltism' of Jerome Bruner (1977), to the extreme latitudinarianism of Carl Rogers (1969). It might seem that liberal humanism might identify most readily with Rogers's 'freedom to learn' as offering an image of the person freely deciding upon a line of enquiry and becoming personally enriched by the commitment undertaken. But this would be to over-simplify. If certain types of knowledge and skill are best acquired by the systematic use of a stimulus–response (S–R) model, then it is wise to use that model for that purpose.

Skinner's theories, which nourish much practice in programmed learning (including computer assisted learning, CAL), can provide liberation for the person who enjoys the privacy of practising skills with a machine rather than in (the perhaps unnecessary) transaction with other people. Some children, for example, are clearly more at ease with *Speak and Spell* and *The Little Professor* (relatively cheap electronic learning aids) than with parents or teachers; computers, after all, never get cross or have headaches. Unfortunately (for educational theory that is), higher education is only minimally concerned with the development of basic skills; it is much more concerned with the higher-level objectives (analysis, synthesis etc.) given in B. S. Bloom's *Taxonomy of Educational Objectives* (1956). These objectives are 'higher' only in the technical sense (involving greater levels of generality and abstraction), not in a 'moral' sense, although we often perversely equate abstraction with virtue.

It is not possible to teach without implicitly (if not explicitly) adopting some or other theory of learning. Many lecturers who profess themselves uninterested in learning theory, in practice adopt (possibly by imitating what they themselves have experienced as students) a crude variant of the S–R theory, the 'jugs-and-mugs' theory (students being seen as vessels to be filled), or even the 'avalanche' theory (as one colleague put it, 'you fling as much stuff as possible at the students, and some of it is bound to stick!')

The common theme in some of the worst practice in the area of university teaching is to assume that the focus of attention should be on *what lecturers do*, rather than on *how students learn*. This is a dangerous emphasis because it is difficult if not impossible to demonstrate a direct link between a specific teaching input and a given learning outcome. Certainly it is possible to list conditions that are *necessary*, such as that students must have access to books, that lecturers should be audible or that students should not be so overwhelmed with material that they do not have time to think about it; but it is not possible to state with certainty what are the *sufficient* conditions to produce effective student learning. Research in teaching methods tends to be somewhat crude; research on student learning is more sophisticated.

A few words are required to explain this apparent pessimism about the possibilities of enlightenment from research on teaching methods. One could, perhaps, if confronted by a totally reductionist position (arguing a mechanistic theory of education based on hypotheses about brain function), invoke Heisenberg's Uncertainty Principle: one cannot (to put it crudely) stop an electron and look at it. The process of observation drastically changes that which is to be observed so that no theory of learning based on fundamental-particle biophysics can ever be attained. One does not, however, need to go back to brain research to encounter the dilemma. Even conventional comparative research has been seriously questioned for some time.

Parlett (in Tawney, 1976) and Hamilton *et al.* (1977) have coined the phrase 'agricultural-botany paradigm' to describe the assumptions underlying much educational research. Hamilton *et al.* (1977), for example, write:

> The most common form of agricultural-botany-type evaluation is presented as an assessment of the effectiveness of an innovation by examining whether or not it has reached required standards on pre-specified criteria. Students – rather like plants – are given pretests (the seedlings are weighed or measured) and then submitted to different experiences (treatment conditions). Subsequently, after a period of time, their attainment (growth or yield) is measured to indicate the relative efficiency of the methods (fertilizers) used. Studies of this kind are designed to yield data of one particular type, i.e. 'objective' numerical data that permit statistical analysis.

There are obvious deficiencies in this type of procedure when it is applied to real-life situations as opposed to 'laboratory' situations in which all or most of the significant variables can be controlled. Indeed, one might wonder whether people's behaviour in social psychology laboratories has any resemblance at all to their behaviour elsewhere! With innovations in teaching methods in higher education, it is particularly hard to control all the variables that might affect the outcome of an experiment (see Goodlad, 1979: 70–7; Goodlad and Hirst, 1989: Chapter 4).

One might, for example, expect the effectiveness of a teaching method (say, group tutorials or seminars) to depend on *inter alia*: the duration of the seminar course; the frequency of the seminars; the duration of each seminar; the differences in age, experience, educational attainment and so on of the students; the amount of experience and training in group teaching methods enjoyed by the lecturer; and possibly also in differences in sex, socio-economic class, ethnic background and so on of lecturer and students. For all practical purposes, it is simply not possible to disentangle all these factors to see which has the most salient influence on the learning of the students.

If one does cross-group or cross-institution comparisons (to enlarge sample sizes) one runs into another set of problems (similar to those affecting 'impact studies': see Chapter 2) concerning the differences between institutions (or departments within them) whose students may have selected them, or been selected for them, according to principles which make the comparison of institutions of doubtful validity.

There are other technical difficulties which diminish confidence in the possible value of comparative studies of teaching methods even within individual educating institutions. If one is doubtful about the wisdom of generalizing from the results of specifically contrived 'laboratory' research, one is left with the possibility of some kind of 'action' research – using students who are studying for their degrees.

First, there is the problem of research ethics. Can one justify using degree studies as the substance of research without telling the students? If one does tell the students, might they not (legitimately) claim that if the research hypothesis holds that one method (say seminars) was believed to be better than another (lectures), all students should be exposed to the method most likely to be fruitful? One certainly cannot permit volunteers; volunteer bias is one of the best known hazards of social science research.

Second, ideally one should compare x hours of one method (seminars) offered to an experimental group with x hours of the other method (lectures) offered to a control group. But what if students from either the seminar group or the control group want to raise questions with the lecturer after sessions? Is one to control the very kind of transactions which higher education seeks to stimulate?

Third, to preserve the purity of an experimental design, one might wish to keep experimental and control groups apart so that the effects that one is trying to measure for the 'seminar' group do not 'bleed across' to the 'lecture' group by informal interaction between students. Quite apart from the fact that in practice one might hope that the beneficial effects of an educational innovation will spread as widely as possible as quickly as possible, it is simply not possible to keep participants in educational experiments in cocoons or in 'quarantine' like jurors in a murder trial. The long-term effects of experiments in teaching methods are, for all practical purposes, impossible to measure.

The implications of this uncertainty are important: if one cannot be sure that a teaching method is positively helpful to students, one should be cautious in promoting it. Uncertainty does not, however, imply inaction: one can be certain about uncertainty. In other words, one can let the very uncertainty that might seem damaging to a *dirigiste* theory of education become the sustaining principle of a liberal humanist one.

If one is uncertain about the effect of a teaching method, it is probably wise always to strive for the greatest degree possible of explicitness in transactions with students, explaining what is hoped for from the activity recommended and enlisting students' cooperation. Such a posture does not involve continuous dialogue, any more than one would expect a surgeon, having explained the desirability of an operation and acquired the patient's consent, to consult the patient about every movement of his hand. However, just as an element of self-consciously critical 'migration' is desirable in the curriculum so that assumptions may be seen for what they are, so an element of transaction, of mutuality, of dialogue, needs to permeate teaching methods, so that teacher and taught can relate as responsible, independent adults.

The respect for persons implied in the position being advanced in this book implies a preference not only for sharing with students one's thinking about the deep structure and organizing principles of a discipline, but also for sharing one's thinking about the way in which various learning procedures are designed to assist the students in becoming acquainted with the deep structure – and also with routine techniques that may be necessary for professional practice. In short, what is required is an orientation towards *assisting students with their learning*, rather than (although this is a somewhat artificial contrast) a commitment to a specific set of 'teaching' techniques. This may require university lecturers to be explicit with students regarding what they believe to be the most effective processes of learning. This certainly does *not* involve telling the students a series of tricks and tips of 'study skills'. Rather, it requires some sort of meta-analysis of the nature of the discipline in question and a sharing of insights into the range of procedures that may help students to attain the necessary knowledge.

By good fortune, such an approach, which is here justified on humanistic grounds rather than psychological grounds, is consistent with what is known about student learning. Here, the research is a surer guide to what is sensible. While it is hard to be confident about research studies concerning specific teaching methods, because they usually involve comparisons that are not legitimate, one can be reasonably confident about what are sensible learning procedures for students to adopt.

Entwistle and Marton (1984), and Entwistle more recently (Entwistle, 1992) have conveniently summarized a style of educational research to which

Marton (1981) has given the name phenomenography. Experiments in Gothenburg by Marton and his colleagues (Marton and Saljo, 1976, 1984) found differences in the ways in which students went about their studying. Asked to read an academic article, and to be ready to answer questions on it afterwards, some students concentrated on trying to identify key facts and ideas on which they expected to be questioned afterwards. Marton called this the *surface approach* to learning. Other students, by contrast, tried to understand the evidence and judge the argument, using what Marton called a *deep approach* – one more like that which university teachers often like to think they encourage. Subsequent research showed that students who used the deep approach tended to be more successful in their studies than the students who used the surface approach, even when the examinations tested factual recall.

Other research in the 1970s and 1980s (Laurillard, 1979, 1987; Entwistle and Ramsden, 1983) revealed that students adopted varying techniques in studying, and that these were closely related to content. Ramsden (1987) argued for a 'relational perspective' which would conceptualize the teaching and learning process holistically, inquiring into how students learned specific subject matter in particular contexts. More recently, the researches of Meyer among others (see Meyer and Muller, 1990; Meyer and Watson, 1991) showed that there was a connection between how students learned and the perceived environment – particularly that if students felt overburdened with work and harassed by assessment, they tended to adopt unfruitful surface approaches to studying. In short, although it is still not possible to demonstrate the *sufficient* conditions to encourage effective learning, one can be more certain about what it is necessary to *avoid*.

From a review of the research on student learning, Marton and Ramsden (1988) suggest a number of teaching strategies that are wholly consonant with the humanist perspective being advanced in this book: (a) make the learners' conceptions explicit to them; (b) focus on a few critical issues and show how they relate; (c) highlight the inconsistencies within and the consequences of learners' conceptions; (d) create situations where learners centre attention on relevant aspects; (e) present the learner with new ways of seeing; (f) integrate substantive and syntactic structures, i.e. to teach 'knowing how' alongside 'knowing that'; (g) test understanding of phenomena and use the results for diagnostic assessment and curriculum design; (h) use reflective teaching strategies.

From this perspective, the 'good teacher' is not necessarily the person capable of charismatic performances in the lecture theatre (important though this may be in stimulating initial interest) or the person so knowledgeable as to be able to give a 'helicopter view' of the disciplinary terrain (important though this is as well). Rather, university teachers need to be familiar with the research on student learning so as to reinforce their students' learning and lead them to the deep structures of ideas (rather than to generate the surface approach) – and also to be aware of the heresies into which they can easily slide if due care is not taken.

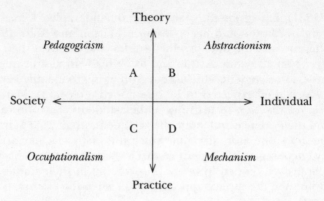

Figure 4.1 The heresies of teaching methods.

Heresies

The heresies which affect teaching methods (see Figure 4.1) are very similar to those which affect curriculum – not surprisingly, because form and content are inextricably intertwined.

Heresy 5: Pedagogicism (A)

Over-planning of education, or over-dependence on some theory of learning, to the extent that the provisional and tentative nature of educational theory is lost to sight.

Curriculum design by objectives is an activity prone to this heresy. Pedagogicism is in this segment because the seeming rationality of listing learning and teaching objectives is the classic stuff of curriculum committees, audit and assessment groups and so forth established to ensure the (entirely proper) accountability of educators to those who pay their salaries. The contrast is, of course, the *atelier* or apprentice model in which the student learns by direct observation of an expert and by being given small tasks of gradually increasing complexity.

The fundamental premise of the approach involving course-design by objectives (as advocated by, for example, Rowntree, 1988) is that what students are to learn should be specified precisely in terms of what they should be able to *do* as a result of having undertaken the necessary learning. For example, my *aim* in writing this paragraph is to alert you to one danger of curriculum planning. My *objective* for you is that you should be able to describe the difference between an aim and an objective, evaluate a curriculum design in terms of achievable objectives and avoid specifying tasks for students that are too rigid. That is to say, my aim is a broad description of intention; the objectives are concrete, behavioural, precise – and capable of being tested.

All this is admirable, and entirely consonant with the attempt to draw students into an understanding of what their studies are for. However, there is an implicit reductionism in this approach embedded in the assumption that one can decide in advance precisely what is to be learned and how it is to be tested. Admirable though this approach may be for training, and for the inculcation of low-level skills, it is ever in danger of being at variance with the tentativeness and 'authoritative uncertainty' that is at the heart of the academic enterprise. In short, to use an objectives approach to the exclusion of looser, more tentative approaches to the teaching–learning dialogue would be to slide into the heresy of pedagogicism.

Heresy 6: Abstractionism (B)

Over-emphasis on systems of thought, concepts, intellectual structures, to the neglect of the contextual details which alone can give them meaning.

Abstractionism is informed by the valid notion (examined in Chapter 3) that a major, if not *the* major, contribution of academic disciplines to our understanding of the world is the power of their organizing concepts, the acceleration to learning that these concepts can bring about. Disciplines bring order by limiting the field and method of observation.

It is easy to slide into the belief that the concepts are in some way 'better' than the details they help us to comprehend, even that the people who analyse, classify and observe are in some ways more noble than those who produce, initiate and do. While it is hard to conceive of education which does not involve abstracting ideas from detail, education which concentrates exclusively on this should be avoided.

Abstractionism is located in segment B because the apparatus of scholarship has a certain identity-giving function for individual practitioners. Just as uniforms are rightly worn with pride by the police, the armed services, paramedics and members of numerous occupations, so the capacity to manipulate concepts is a mark of the skilled university teacher. Indeed, to attach one's name to a constant or a law (such as Ohm's law) is to achieve a kind of immortality. It is understandable, though often regrettable, that academics over-emphasize in their teaching the abstractions by which they make sense of the everyday world.

Heresy 7: Occupationalism (C)

Over-emphasis on the practical 'needs of society' (or industry) or the 'demands of the discipline' in specifying the types of learning to be undertaken.

Occupationalism in teaching methods is, of course, superficially similar to the heresy of utilitarianism which affects curriculum: the difference is that the very *techniques* of research, scholarship and reflection through which the content or curriculum are organized, and which are the tools of trade of the academic occupation, become valued for their own sake. As soon as the needs of the (socially constructed) discipline become the overt focus for concern, a heresy is at hand.

Occupationalism is similar in one sense to abstractionism in that both involve identity; the difference is that whereas abstractionism drives towards ways in which the individual teacher rises above the discipline or sub-discipline in offering new perspectives through innovative concepts, occupationalism emphasizes the solidarity of the discipline. It becomes inconceivable that anyone should achieve a degree who has not jumped through the same hoops as the designers of the course. Squires (1990: 107) has suggested that, in the United Kingdom, many courses seem designed primarily as preparation for entry to the *academic profession.* They often conform to the conventional pattern of the apprenticeship, with their carefully graduated stages (apprentice, journeyman, master), their strict job demarcations, the emphasis on personal contact and role modelling, the gradual increase in responsibility, the mimicking of the activity of research in seminars, and library and project work.

Symptoms of the heresy of occupationalism are found occasionally in talk of the need for 'rigour', as though that were an end in itself and not the means towards some other end, not as yet defined.

Heresy 8: Mechanism (D)

The vice of treating persons as part of some system or organization, neglecting other dimensions of their personality.

Whereas survivalism is the heresy whereby individual students over-value education for supposedly supplying job skills (and thereby collude, wittingly or unwittingly, with those whose heresy is utilitarianism), mechanism is in quadrant D as the characteristic vice of manpower planners and trainers of one sort or another. There is nothing intrinsically wrong with training: we need to submit to the prescriptions of those who have mastered techniques if we are to learn the techniques ourselves. Heresy creeps in when techniques become the primary object of education.

Mechanism is, perhaps, most visible in vocational, technical education. If students are treated only as intending engineers, physicists or whatever, with no encouragement or opportunity to develop any other interests in their studies, they are being treated as means to some other end (supplying the manpower 'needs of industry', for example) rather than as persons. Mechanism, though less visible, is, however, present in the humanities too. If scholarship or research become reified ('historical research requires...', 'Patagonian studies require...'), people in higher education can slip into the heresy of forgetting what is the purpose of their work, letting work become the purpose of their lives.

The fact that mechanism often uses the language of fluid dynamics ('the flow of candidates', 'new blood' etc.), rather than that of straight mechanics ('force', 'momentum' etc.), should not disguise its dehumanizing quality and fundamental illiberality.

Preferences

As already indicated, liberal humanist preferences in this area necessarily involve a search for the possibility of mutuality and debate, of two-way transaction (in which lecturer and student learn from each other, and take one another's preoccupations seriously), rather than the *de haut en bas* posture of the teacher controlling the activity of the learner according to some plan of which the learner is left in ignorance.

It would be naive to assume that, particularly in the area of professional education where many constraints are imposed on universities by the requirements of professional accrediting bodies, there is always substantial room for negotiation about detailed content. There may, however, be much merit in allowing substantial negotiation of content – not least because scientists are often valued by employers as much for their generalized competence in the design and execution of complex experiments as for their detailed knowledge of specific facts, and engineers, likewise, will ultimately be managers of projects as much as repositories of specific technical information. In both cases, the *process* by which the students have acquired their knowledge may be as important as, even more important than, the particular product of knowledge that they represent.

Negotiating the framework: personalized systems of instruction

It may sound hopelessly Utopian to suggest some process of consultation between teachers and taught at the beginning of their acquaintanceship: how could the timetable, allocation of rooms, library purchases and so on possibly be arranged if this were to take place? Is it not sufficient that students can make 'market' choices between institutions and courses (whose operating style they can discover from a multitude of 'consumer' guides) before they apply? Perhaps: but consultation is a form of courtesy that needs to be extended whenever and wherever there is any room at all for manoeuvre. In most courses in higher education, there is very considerable room for manoeuvre.

In Chapter 3, mention was made of the degree by independent study available at the University of East London (formerly East London Polytechnic). This degree not only permits and encourages independent choice by the student of the content of the degree (within the limits of what the university can offer), but also encourages a modicum of choice within learning and assessment methods, the students being permitted (within broad guide-lines) to decide *how* as well as *what* they will study.

One very important component of 'how' is the pacing and timing of study. One symptom of the heresy of pedagogicism is the use of teaching methods which depend too much on the presence and performance of the lecturer. Indeed, many systems of academic accountancy in educational bureaucracies rely, misguidedly, on 'class contact' as the basis of currency. If such 'class contact' constrains all the students to do the same thing at the same time, then a nonsense is being perpetrated. 'Class contact' can, how-ever, be combined with considerable freedom for students by the use of personalized systems of instruction (PSI), such as Keller plan courses which require mastery of one module before the next can be undertaken. Such courses, which have been used successfully in a wide variety of disciplines (see Johnston, 1975; Kulik and Kulik, 1976), are often effectively 'corre-spondence courses taken in-house' and can be readily adapted to be taken in either internal or external mode.

It goes almost without saying that any part of a degree programme should provide sufficient information for students that they may see *why* any indi-vidual part is there and what to do to achieve competence. If a subject, such as engineering, requires complete mastery of specific material, it is proper that students should be told this and then put in a position to achieve that mastery. In such conditions, PSI methods become not only desirable but, perhaps, even essential. The basic features of a PSI course are admirably summarized by Keller, one of the pioneers of this type of instruction:

(1) The go-at-your-own-pace feature, which permits a student to move through the course at a speed commensurate with his [*sic*] ability and other demands upon his time.

(2) The unit-completion requirement for advance, which lets the stu-dent go ahead to new material only after demonstrating mastery of that which preceded.

(3) The use of lectures and demonstrations as vehicles of motivation, rather than as sources of critical information.

(4) The related stress upon the written word in teacher-student com-munications; and finally:

(5) The use of proctors which permits repeated testing, immediate scoring, almost unavoidable tutoring, and a marked enhancement of the personal–social aspect of the educational process.

(Keller, 1968: 83)

Courses in science embodying these features have been used in the United Kingdom both at school level (see Daly and Robertson, 1978) and in the Higher Education Learning Project (Physics) sponsored by the Nuffield Foundation (see Bridge and Elton, 1977).

Research (mostly conducted in the 1970s) suggests that PSI courses are both popular with students and effective in encouraging student learning.

For example, in an analysis based only on studies systematically comparing PSI with other types of instruction, Taveggia concluded that,

When evaluated by average student performance on course content examinations, the Personalized System of Instruction has proved superior to the conventional teaching methods with which it has been compared. Not one of the independent comparisons of PSI with conventional methods favors the conventional methods. This is irrespective of the type of course in which the study was conducted (e.g. physical science, natural science, social science, engineering), or the type of conventional method with which PSI was compared (e.g. lecture, lecture-discussion, group discussion).

(Taveggia, 1976: 1029)

In a meta-analysis of seventy-five comparative studies, Kulik, Kulik and Cohen (1979) come to a similar conclusion.

Although I have recommended a healthy scepticism about the comparison of teaching methods, these findings merit note. Particularly do they merit note when they focus on the efficiency and effectiveness of *student learning*, rather than on the specifics of the performance of teachers.

In a review study concentrating specifically on the use of Keller plan in science teaching, Kulik *et al.* (1974) found that the Keller plan method is a method attractive to most students. In every published report that they examined, students rated the Keller plan much more favourably than teaching by lecture. Secondly, self-pacing and interaction with tutors seemed to be the features of the Keller courses most favoured by students. Although several of the investigations reviewed by Kulik *et al.* (1974) reported higher-than-average withdrawal rates from the Keller courses than from conventional courses, it seems possible to control both withdrawal and a related problem of student procrastination through course design. Hursh (1976: 98) reports a number of measures which have been found to prevent procrastination.

Content learning (as measured by final examinations) is adequate in Keller courses. In the published studies reviewed by Kulik *et al.* (1974), final examination performance in Keller courses always equalled, and usually exceeded, performance in lecture courses. More importantly, students reported that they learned more in PSI than in lecture courses, and nearly always put more time and effort into the Keller courses. A similar study by Aiello and Wolfle (1980) supports these observations.

Two of the features of Keller plan courses seem particularly attractive to students, and are important for the purposes of the present argument. The first is self-pacing. Robin (1976: 343) sees this as one of the keys to the proven effectiveness of PSI. If university departments used PSI for the core material in degree courses (that is, the material which is the irreducible minimum of what students should know), this would offer students a highly desirable element of flexibility. Absence through illness is a severe problem in many hard-packed science and engineering lecture courses: if students miss lectures through illness, they can run the risk of never catching up. With Keller plan courses, not only is this danger avoided, but students can get more control over their own study through self-pacing and, most importantly, see the overall structure of the course as they go along.

The second is proctoring. One classic difficulty in university teaching is that the frame of reference of lecturers, through the simple fact of their greater experience in the subject, is often radically different from (and usually technically superior to) that of the students. Sometimes, it is easier for students to learn from people who are nearer to them in age and experience than from people who are much more experienced – and with whom students sometimes experience feelings of undue deference and even anxiety.

The use of students to help students, which is a regular feature of Keller plan courses, has benefits in this area. Students who lack confidence can derive significant support from other students. Hursh (1976: 101) reports that the combination of this with study groups has proved highly effective. A group of students has to take quizzes and have them graded by a proctor at one time and is not permitted to advance to the next unit until all three members of the group have passed the current quiz. This version of PSI results in fewer withdrawals than regular PSI, and examination scores, grades and ratings that are higher than those from the lecture sessions but similar to the grades and ratings of PSI courses. Proctoring has proved popular in conventionally taught engineering courses (see Button *et al.*, 1990). Combined with study groups, it has the potential to release the massive benefits known to be associated with many forms of peer tutoring (see Goodlad and Hirst, 1989).

Courses run in this way provide the opportunity for students not only to negotiate the framework of time, but also, through interaction with their peers, to negotiate the intellectual framework as well. It is this exposure to the fundamental organizing concepts of the discipline and the rationale for the teaching methods used that makes such approaches consonant with the perspective advanced in this book.

Project methods

In Chapter 3, I argue that project methods offer one method of achieving reflexivity in the *content* of the curriculum. Project methods are also attractive logistically as a *method* of achieving flexibility in teaching.

One conventional approach to achieving liberality in the curriculum is for a university to offer a multiplicity of taught options, usually in the final year of study. This can, however, be extremely expensive in staff time, particularly if specific options attract only a handful of students. If lecturers already have the background knowledge from which to propose and offer a lecture course, they are *ipso facto* equipped to supervise project work in those areas. More importantly, if initiative is given to students in the formulation of a project brief, a student can draw upon the help of more than one lecturer. Project methods, as I have argued at length elsewhere (Goodlad, 1975b), have other attractions.

First, they not only make learning active, rather than passive, but also, like independent study, encourage students to take more responsibility for their own education.

Second, project methods, as hinted above, permit and encourage students to combine knowledge from different disciplinary traditions. Even (perhaps especially) in joint-honours or modular courses, it may be difficult for the parts to be effectively welded together: integration must take place in the mind of the student, who may need somewhat elaborate counselling to find an academically coherent way through all that is on offer (see Watson *et al.*, 1989). Project methods can be the means whereby such integration is achieved.

Third, project methods allow a student to look deeply into a field of knowledge. In theory, single-subject honours courses have this as their primary object; however, it is often students' experience that the unity of the subject dissolves into a congeries of bits and pieces, topics covered separately in a multitude of required courses with never enough time being allowed for them to pursue a subject in depth. If depth of knowledge leads to the feeling of mastery, and mastery to the confidence to learn on one's own, project methods are a desirable means to an important end.

Fourth, project methods, in addition to providing logistic flexibility to a department, recognize the different speeds at which students study – recognizing that some students think deeply but not quickly, a quality not recognized in three-hour examinations.

Socio-technical projects in engineering education

As a case study, I will describe briefly a type of project work which I was involved in starting in the Electrical Engineering Department of Imperial College in 1963, and which became the preferred model for the General Education in Engineering project, chaired by Dr David Brancher and funded by the Nuffield Foundation (see Goodlad, 1977).

One of the well-known difficulties about providing, within engineering education, additive courses in the humanities and social sciences is that students may never make, because they are not given the opportunity to make, effective connections between the different types of knowledge that they are acquiring. In medical education, and in some other fields, problem-based learning has been developed as a response to the situation (see Chapter 3). An intermediate arrangement, as it were, is to make *part* of the degree course problem-based with a view to sewing together some of the material dealt with in a discursive manner elsewhere.

Early on in the development of humanities options for students at Imperial College (see Chapter 3), the need was experienced for an activity that would attempt to bring about this merging of questions concerning *how* (the stuff of engineering) with questions concerning *why* and *whether* (the stuff of the humanities). In the Electrical Engineering Department, which under Professor Sir Willis Jackson and Professor Arnold Tustin pioneered the introduction of humanities courses at Imperial College, all students were able to take options in the humanities, social sciences and languages. In addition, all third-year (final-year at that time) students undertook group projects in groups of five or six under the supervision and direction of members of the engineering staff. The project groups studied engineering questions that were made complicated by the presence of significant economic, political or social factors, or studied social, political or economic issues important to the engineering profession.

Topics studied in the early projects included: the likely effects upon the electricity supply industry of the discovery of oil in the North Sea; the economic and social effects of the progress of automation in selected sectors of British industry; the feasibility of automatic control of civil aircraft in Europe; the possible causes of, and remedies for, 'motorway madness'.

A modification of this scheme was the provision for some students of overseas group projects. Three factors influenced the decision to mount such projects. First, there was difficulty in fitting into the crowded timetable of the third year projects of sufficient complexity to command the interest of students and yet not leave them disheartened by finding (as they usually did) that the subject area was already filled with active researchers. Second, some students were having unsatisfactory experiences of industry during their vacation training, particular in the second long vacation, when industry often did not seem to know what to do with them. Third, it seemed highly desirable that students should become aware of the ways in which British industry marketed technical systems abroad. Fourth, and relatedly, it seemed valuable to give engineers who would spend a significant part of their lives designing things some insight into how equipment was installed and maintained abroad.

Accordingly, conversations were started with a number of universities overseas with a view to setting up group projects to be carried out jointly by the Imperial College students and the students from the host countries. One of the first of these projects involved the installation of rural electrification in an area of Sierra Leone (see Goodlad, 1970). Four Imperial College electrical engineering students joined one civil engineering student and one mechanical engineering student from Fourah Bay College; they spent seven weeks during the summer vacation of 1968 at Ywfin, a township and mission station in the north-east of Sierra Leone, carrying out work on the mission's electrical supply. They installed a 15kVa diesel generator and made a suitable switchboard; erected a 600-yard overhead transmission line to the mission's bible school and hospital compound, and an 800-yard overhead line to the courthouse and the paramount chief's house in the town; and carried out a feasibility study for a small hydro scheme on a nearby stream. The students studied the overall provision of electricity supply in Sierra Leone and tried to assess the main requirements for the complete electrification of Ywfin within the context of the developing electricity supply of the country at large.

In addition to gaining very valuable practical experience, the students learned a great deal about the economic problems facing a small town in an African country, and a great deal about themselves – in terms of the type of engineering they might wish to become involved with in their careers.

Subsequent overseas group projects involved students in work on rural electrification in Zambia, on telecommunications work in Venezuela and in assisting with a UNESCO health-education scheme in Tunisia (by designing and building a robust tape-playing device for use with exhibitions) (Brown and Goodlad, 1971).

There are obvious difficulties in mounting schemes of this sort. At one time it seemed that an inevitable consequence of a letter from myself to an overseas university was for revolution to break out in the country concerned! More generally, there was the issue of providing adequate supervision of the students' work overseas – although it must be said that the students seemed to flourish *without* any supervision. At about the time when we were considering these matters, I received a telephone call from Alec Dickson, founder of Voluntary Service Overseas and later of Community Service Volunteers. He had read about these projects and put, with his customary bluntness, the question that we were already starting to consider: why were we not doing in the United Kingdom group projects like those overseas, which combined education for the students with work of direct practical utility to other people?

From this stimulus, we started projects that might be called advocacy engineering, where the notion is that student engineers seek to serve the needs of those who would not normally see themselves as the clients of engineers – much as town planning students and law students do through, respectively, advocacy planning and advocacy law. Student engineers can discover and articulate the need for physical systems and devices (and related administrative procedures) of those who are not adequately represented by the political process or appropriately catered for by commerce. By and large, these are people who are mentally or physically handicapped, old, poor or in some other way disadvantaged.

Probably the best time (indeed, it might be the *only* time) that engineers can explore this whole area of work is when they are students. The object of the action-oriented group projects was to enable students to *do work of direct practical utility as part of their curriculum*. Group projects of this type included the study of the Meals-on-Wheels service of a London borough with a view to making improvements in its efficiency and effectiveness (see Goodlad, 1975a: 142–3) and the writing of a proposal for a scheme to help the chronically unemployed, which led to the subsequent opening, with Manpower Services Commission funds, of a sheltered workplace in another London borough (see Goodlad, 1977: 30–2). These action-oriented projects were my first fumbling efforts in what is now known (in UNESCO parlance) as study service or (in US terminology) service learning (see below).

Many of the benefits of socio-technical group projects of this kind can also, however, be acquired by projects where the research outcome is limited to a report alone, rather than the associated designing and building of physical systems. These benefits include:

- the *commitment* that can come from writing a document that may lead to some action;
- the experience of *initiative* involved in taking a loosely defined issue and deciding what engineers can do about it by way of designing physical systems;
- the experience of *cooperation* involved in carrying out a project as part of a group;
- relatedly, the development of *communication skills*, not only in running meetings, writing letters, carrying out interviews and giving spoken presentations, but also in writing a report with a specific client in view, (rather than the somewhat deadening experience of writing laboratory reports for the person who set up the laboratory in the first place);
- acquiring *knowledge of the organization of knowledge* by carrying out literature searches with a view to narrowing a field down to the point at which specific material can be located;
- the *sense of responsibility* that can arise from trying to contribute to professional debate on an issue.

I well remember the satisfaction of a project group examining the question, 'Is lead in petrol a hazard to health? If it is, who should do what about it?' when, having sent their project report via an MP to the Minister of Transport, they read that the government had proposed measures exactly in line with their recommendations. *Post hoc, ergo propter hoc?*

The General Education in Engineering project sought to promote similar types of project work, by individuals as well as by groups, throughout the United Kingdom. Its initiator, Dr David Brancher, himself a civil engineer and a former member of HMI, was keen to get away from the limitation of engineering problems to small precisely stated matters (important though these are in the education of students): 'calculate the stress . . .', 'devise the formula . . .', 'list the properties of . . .', 'optimize X with respect to Y'. He selected as a broad field for the Nuffield-funded project that of urban problems, and established aims for the students as follows (Brancher, 1975: 37):

- to perceive, grasp, and describe a complex multi dimensional situation, issue or problem;
- to imagine a range of developments, outcomes or solutions;
- to set up appropriate criteria;
- to recognize, make and defend value judgements;
- to see the effects of background and self-image in professional behaviour;
- to work and communicate effectively with others.

Within the broad field of urban problems, projects were carried out in a variety of universities on such topics as:

- Energy – 'the management of fossil fuel resources', 'the harnessing of solar energy', 'a critique of government energy policy', 'an investigation of the relationship between energy and urban transport in the context of future energy supplies'.
- Transport – 'prediction of car ownership', 'a future transport system for inner Birmingham', 'a study of the engineering and environmental implications in the modernization of the lower section of the Grand Union Canal', 'Bicycles and the oil shortage'.
- Urban vulnerability – 'youth and vandalism', 'urban vulnerability to natural disasters such as flooding'.

The most effective projects were those in which students did not attempt too much, and those in which the project built around a core of engineering knowledge but in such a way as to permit and encourage discussion between the students. It obviously helped when, as was usually the case, the supervisor was enthusiastic, and it was important that projects were undertaken in areas where things were happening (rather than in areas which had ceased to be actively studied by others in the field).

Relatedly, projects worked best where there was available an adequate supply of suitable literature; indeed, one of the key skills (that of the students finding their way through the literature) depended on this. Likewise, when students had worked their way into a subject, and before they started to despair at the mountains of material available and the seeming intractability of some of the issues, it proved useful to arrange for some inspirational input, such as a seminar with an invited expert (or a visit by the students to such a person).

Socio-technical projects such as these may seem at variance with the focusing logic of academic disciplines; they are, however, part of the *psycho-logic* of learning the subject of engineering in that they anticipate fruitfully the professional persona that the student will inhabit. In this regard, without making the academic subject matter person-centred, they put the person of the student right at the centre of an area of debate. All the indications were (and are, because such project work continues at Imperial College) that these and similarly oriented activities are highly valued by the students.

Project methods such as those described above should not of course be the *only* method of university education: to suggest that they should would be to be guilty of the heresy of pedagogicism. Properly handled, project methods do, however, offer students the possibility of relating theory to practice, and perhaps thereby of seeing the focusing, organizing power of the concepts of their disciplines. In short, they offer the opportunity to move towards the middle of the theory–practice axis in a way which is fruitfully faithful to the merits of both theory and practice without being suborned by either.

There are, needless to say, numerous other ways in which students can enjoy the sense of engagement that project work engenders. The next section examines some of these, particularly those that use the idea of study service mentioned above.

Engagement–reflection modes of study: study service

To avoid the dangers of heresies on the society–individual axis, a teaching method is required which allows students to see their obligations to themselves (in terms of the nourishment of their imaginations, of their sense of individuality and of their obligations to 'society') in the sense of offering opportunity to relate their studies directly or indirectly to the interests and needs of the community which is paying for those students.

Study service (or service learning as it is called in the USA) is the process through which students combine their personal learning with work which is of direct and tangible benefit to other people (see Goodlad, 1982). Students in study service schemes do not compete with paid professionals; rather, they do work *which could not otherwise have been done.*

In a major examination of study service in the United Kingdom (Whitley, 1980, 1982), Community Service Volunteers distinguished study service from staff consultancy/research on the one hand, and from purely voluntary extra-curricular student activities on the other. Four criteria distinguish study service from other work in which people in higher education serve society:

1 Students (not staff alone) should be involved.
2 The work should be an integral part of the curriculum and preferably assessed.
3 There should normally be direct contact, at some stage of the course, between students and intended beneficiaries.
4 The effect of the work should be detectable at individual or small-group level.

In the United Kingdom, for example (see Goodlad, 1982), law students have given free legal advice to people who cannot afford professional fees; town planning students have helped tenants to formulate and express their views about planning proposals that might affect them; engineering students (as we have seen) have studied the needs of old, poor and disabled people for systems and devices (telephones, meals-on-wheels, sheltered employment) which neither government nor private industry had examined; theology and sociology students have worked in a wide variety of community groups, statutory and voluntary, giving various sorts of practical help; students of languages have taught English to immigrants; and technical college students on day-release have built an adventure playground as part of their liberal studies. In every case, the involvement of the students' teachers has been designed to ensure that the service is *competent* – the basic requirement of all community service. The use of community service as a focus for learning has also ensured *reciprocity* – both students and those whom they seek to serve benefiting in different ways from the activity, which diminishes the likelihood of paternalism on the one hand or exploitation on the other.

Like all forms of work experience and experiential learning, study service requires careful planning and execution. For the academic staff, it can be more adventurous (or more tiresome, depending on how they view it) by involving activities by students which are inevitably outside the immediate direction and control of the academic staff. Although I have noted elsewhere (Goodlad, 1982: Chapter 13) some of the factors to consider when starting a study service programme, I note a few of them here to give a flavour of study service as a teaching technique, and lest anyone anxious to avoid heresy slides instead into muddle.

Identify needs
One of the least satisfactory aspects of conventional work experience is that students are very often not really needed in the places to which they go; indeed, they may actually be a nuisance, the opportunity costs of finding something for them to do being endured by receiving agencies only with a view to the possibility of getting good recruits later. By contrast, study service based on the principle of reciprocity can generate projects that are a unique combination of the opportunities for learning provided by an educating institution and by the social constituency that it serves.

In the conference from which the book *Study Service* (Goodlad, 1982) emerged, Alec Dickson offered as a criterion for judging a study service scheme the question: will one human being other than the student benefit from the student's studies? Each student represents a considerable investment of public finance; indeed, in a sense those students on maintenance grants (however modest these now are) are already 'paid' for the work that they do. Can this investment of public money yield benefits in addition to those of helping the students to accumulate knowledge?

Putting the issue another way, one may ask: is it possible to give students a chance to do something *useful* at each stage of their studies? Indeed, if course designers do not provide opportunities for students to do something useful, may not students lose the desire, if not the capacity, to act effectively later? Goodness knows, there are opportunities without number for volunteer work in most organizations concerned with personal care, to say nothing of organizations needing surveys of one sort and another to be carried out. Likewise, it is inconceivable that students concerned with the performing arts (art, drama, music) should lack audiences or that students studying graphic arts (painting, photography, sculpture) should lack subjects for their art works or sites in which their works can give pleasure.

The process of identifying needs, and discussion between staff and students on whether study service activities are effective in meeting those needs, offers abundant opportunity for all parties to reflect on the meaning and purpose of what they are doing at university.

Recognize the problems

For all its attractions, study service bristles with problems, many of them profound. No one's interests will be served if people undertake study service without anticipating the problems.

I have already stressed that study service should concentrate on work that could not otherwise be done. Although there is no lack of things to be done, everyone concerned with study service needs to beware of the danger of *substitution*, in which tasks undertaken by students in the course of their studies take work away from those who need the work to earn their living. Considerable tact is required in any study service scheme to ensure that everyone whose interests might be involved is consulted.

Second, the notion of *reciprocity* is crucial. The very word 'service' in study service reminds one of the danger of patronizing attitudes developing. It must be clear to all concerned that *mutual* benefits are being sought: for students, an increment in learning, and for those with whom and for whom they work, the performance of necessary tasks. Some study service schemes use 'contracts of expectation' (see Knowles, 1986) to try to identify in advance what everyone involved hopes to gain from a project.

Third, a limiting factor on the spread of study service is likely to be the ability of receiving agencies to *absorb* the numbers of students who could become involved. Not only do educating institutions have to anticipate the costs of people to organize placements and the time needed to liaise with academic staff, so also do they need to recognize that there are opportunity costs for receiving agencies in adjusting routines to make best use of volunteers.

Fourth, and related, is the notion of *complementarity*. Increasingly it is being perceived that the key roles of professional people are the management of systems and the formulation and communication of advice. If these tasks are effectively carried out, lay people will become better able to look after their own health, education and so forth. While professional practices are changing, it is extremely important to assess *how* volunteers can best assist professionals. It goes without saying that the very process of deciding this can be a fruitful part of the education of the students.

Fifth, attention needs to be given to the *reward and promotion system* for the academic staff. A common experience with study service schemes is that the rewards for the students are very clear: the immediate satisfaction of being useful; increments in learning; and highly valuable experience to report to potential employers. However, the reward system for the academic staff depends at present primarily upon a record of refereed publications. So far, this problem has not been cracked – even by the Enterprise in Higher Education initiative of the Department of Employment, which has some similarity to the study service movement.

Define aims

The phrase study service implies twin objectives: of academic study and practical service. If activities are not to fall apart administratively, it is important to confront two key questions: (a) study for what; (b) service for what?

	In here	Out there
Students		
Teachers		
Others		

Figure 4.2 An aid to identify what you are doing and why.

The 'contracts of expectation' referred to above are designed to record what all parties to a study service arrangement are hoping to gain. They are not easy to write! Indeed, the process of thinking through in advance what is to be done and why can be immensely fruitful in its own right. Ron Johnson suggested (Goodlad, 1982: 208) the diagram shown in Figure 4.2 as an aid for everyone to identify what they are doing and why.

'Out there' contexts can provide students with abundant opportunities to ask questions about, for example, how institutions operate, who relates to whom, how and why, where inputs (of raw material, of people, of problems etc.) come from and how outputs are evaluated. Many things can be observed on placements that cannot readily be simulated in educating institutions; but they may not be observed unless students are trained to look. It is important to be as clear as possible not only about what service is to be rendered to whom through the study service activity, but also about what the student is expected to learn through rendering the service – and how the anticipated learning fits in with the university teacher's aims and objectives in running the course of which the study service is a part.

The types of enrichment that study service can offer can involve not only knowledge and skills relevant to professional formation, but also those relevant to personal growth. As Arthur Chickering pointed out (Goodlad, 1982: 209), adult students may not have the same need for, or expectations from, study service activity as students coming straight from school. Typically, he pointed out, adults are experience-rich but theory-poor; by contrast, school-leaver students are often theory-rich but experience-poor. The aims of specific study service collaborations need to be formulated very carefully to accommodate the specific needs of all involved.

Likewise, objectives need to be *appropriate*. To harmonize with the operating requirements of the 'action agencies' (i.e. the sites where students will be doing their service), the aims may need to be stated in terms of tasks to be carried out. Students' study service experience may then need to be subjected to detailed retrospective analysis to discover what has been learned.

Define roles
As with most forms of project work, a crucial question is: who is to be in control of what is learned? With conventional university project work, negotiation always has to take place on this matter between university teacher

and student. (Indeed, codes of intellectual property rights are currently proliferating in universities.) With study service, the recipient of the student's work is a further party to the arrangement. Ron Johnson suggested that it is desirable for students, teachers and others to be as explicit as possible not only about what is to be done, but also about the expectations each holds of the others.

An important part of the business of defining roles is that of defining the *reward system*; that is, the criteria by which performance of the role will be judged. We have already noted the problem this offers for rewarding the academic staff. It is equally important that students should know what is what. If they are expected to do one thing (render service) but are rewarded only for doing something else (writing essays), role strain is likely to ensue with attendant frustration and disappointment.

Evaluate the students' learning

In study service and related fields of action learning, there continues to be much debate about what should be assessed and how. Certainly the students need *credit* of some sort for the service they give; but should this be in the form of degree marks? Assessment of the action might be valid; but is it likely also to be reliable?

In study service, as in all forms of academic endeavour, it is necessary to distinguish between formative and summative evaluation. Formative evaluation is a form of feedback in which the object is to monitor an activity with a view to improving it as it goes along. Summative evaluation, by contrast, is designed to offer some final judgement as to whether the students have done what is expected of them. Attempts to evaluate students' study service work can be confusing if this distinction is not maintained. Needless to say, there is considerable merit in drawing students into the discussion of what is to be assessed and how – even in encouraging them to *assess themselves*. This very process can help in pointing up the learning to be achieved through the practical activities.

As with independent learning, knowledge of specific facts (important though this is) will probably prove less important for assessment than the development of *personal and professional skills*, including those of defining problems, gathering data systematically, making effective use of a wide range of sources of information, writing clear essays or reports, conducting meetings and giving oral presentations both in the university and in the action agency. Students will benefit the more from study service if their work is not only subjected to retrospective analysis but also planned so as to involve the deployment of the widest possible range of competencies.

Evaluate the programme

Whether or not one wishes to evaluate the performance of individual students taking part in study service, it is always desirable to evaluate as carefully as possible the overall programme of which the students' work is a part.

A '*statement of intent*' for the programme as a whole, as well as 'contracts of expectation' for all those involved, can give a useful sense of direction for an activity. Again, there are significant pedagogic advantages in drawing students into the process of framing such a statement, or revising it regularly if the programme continues from academic year to academic year.

Abundant *record keeping* not only can provide raw material with which to evaluate a programme, but can also help with the education of students. Information about, for example, units of activity per pound invested, number of contacts, number of specific actions taken and so forth does not necessarily tell one whether a study service programme is worthwhile or not; however, it would certainly be difficult to arrive at a judgement *without* relevant information.

Frequent *reports on the programme as a whole*, whether or not written by students, serve two other important functions: (a) they can be used as documents to keep everyone involved informed about what is going on; and (b), relatedly, they can provide continuity from year to year – particularly important if there are changes in staffing either at the university or at the action agency.

What should be apparent from the above notes is that engagement–reflection modes of study, of which study service is but one example, require a type of teaching procedure unlike the more familiar lecture–tutorial mode. Much more of the university teacher's time is involved in *planning and assessing* than in face-to-face instruction. The university teacher becomes more a manager and source of professional wisdom than a purveyor of information.

It is obviously difficult to compare this type of teaching systematically with other types of teaching because one is not comparing like with like. My reason for dwelling at length on the specifics of the method is, rather, to show that procedures can be used which aim at the centre of Figure 4.1, and thereby seek to avoid the nest of heresies associated with teaching methods. The case may be more fully made if I offer some more detail on a specific example of study service: student tutoring.

Student tutoring as a form of study service

One form of study service currently growing in popularity is that of student tutoring (see Goodlad and Hirst, 1989, 1990). In a scheme known as 'The Pimlico Connection', students from Imperial College visit local schools for one afternoon per week for fifteen weeks in the autumn and spring terms. Named after the first school to join the scheme, with twelve tutors in 1975, the scheme has continued to grow. Currently some 180 tutors are in action in seventeen local schools. The students' task is to help teachers with the lessons. The students are not substitute teachers (and they do not teach whole classes); rather, they are a resource to be deployed by teachers as they see fit.

Researches carried out throughout the life of the scheme have shown that *inter alia*: teachers value the help of the tutors in enlivening their lessons and offering positive role models to the pupils; the pupils find the lessons more interesting than normal lessons and feel that they learn more; the student tutors benefit by gaining demanding practice in the communication of scientific ideas and by increasing their self-confidence. Some tutors (though not all, because the scheme is a straight service activity as well as a study service activity) take the opportunity for academic reflection offered by a course in the humanities programme on the communication of scientific ideas.

One attraction of study service schemes is that of offering participating students the opportunity to see a possible career activity from the vantage-point of someone actively involved, rather than as a passive observer. In this regard, it is noteworthy that, over the years, significant numbers of Imperial College tutors have been attracted into teaching – two being attracted into teaching for every one put off the idea. (That some students are put off teaching is no bad thing: it would be very damaging both personally and professionally for students to discover half-way through a PGCE course that teaching was not for them!) In the light of the research information about career choices, in 1987 Imperial College received 'special initiatives' funding from the (then) University Grants Committee to disseminate information about the scheme. Subsequently, British Petroleum provided funds (1990–3) for a three-year fellowship (held by Mr John C. Hughes) to promote the idea nationally.

Following these initiatives, schemes modelled on 'The Pimlico Connection' are now run in 180 other UK universities and FE colleges. In 1992, the Lord Mayor of London, Sir Brian Jenkins, made student tutoring the subject of his national appeal organized by Community Service Volunteers (CSV). With the funds so raised, CSV will become the national centre for information about student tutoring. Imperial College, while continuing to run 'The Pimlico Connection', is exploring new dimensions of student tutoring – such as the pros and cons of students acting as volunteer guides or interpreters in science museums and science centres.

The opportunities for learning from student tutoring are numerous: Goodlad and Hughes (1992) have listed some of the questions to which student tutors might attend *inter alia*: How does the science that the school pupils are studying relate either to the fundamental structure of the scientific discipline or to the world picture of the pupils or both? Why is it that the offspring of professional workers are so much more successful in the UK educational system than the offspring of other social groups? Should education be specifically adapted to the interest and needs of a multicultural community? What other influences, such as television, are at work on the pupils and how does this influence their thinking? Where has the school curriculum come from? Who controls what is done in schools – both strategically and routinely on a day-to-day basis – and on what authority do they exercise their control? If pupils perform differently in their scientific studies, why is this? Are there, for example, differences in intelligence that can be separated out from differences in application, dedication and experience?

Questions such as these give meaning and purpose to theoretical studies that might otherwise seem unrelated to the students' felt needs. Indeed, it is possible (even probable) that students who experience the full intellectual impact of such questions will find the college or university component of a PGCE course almost too short compared with the school-based experience so strongly pressed for at present by government in the United Kingdom.

A 4, 3, 2, 1 approach to university education?

The preceding sections may seem to have over-emphasized independent modes of study at the expense of more familiar, discipline-based study on which most university courses are at present based. Accordingly, I offer here a few thoughts on how a degree course may be conceptualized to accommodate some of the measures I have advocated. Again, because my experience is principally with contributions to science and engineering courses, I will use them as a focus (cf. Goodlad, 1990a).

The 4, 3, 2, 1 approach in the heading of this section refers to a way of considering *core and contextualizing* components of a course. There is, of course, nothing strikingly original about this type of approach; a core-and-context approach was, for example, used when the University of Sussex was founded (see Daiches 1964). The difference is, perhaps, that the 4, 3, 2, 1 approach concentrates on method whereas earlier approaches have been primarily concerned with content.

The approach starts from the observation that in many science and engineering departments (as in other departments in universities) it is possible for a student to achieve a third-class degree for a mark of 40 per cent. The implication of this is that there is an irreducible minimum of material, constituting 40 per cent of what a student *could* know, that the university has decided the student *should* know to achieve honours. In practice, one suspects (indeed, knows from personal observation) that students working at this level may not know anything very well at all. Might it not be better that all students knew *some* material very, very well indeed – in short, that they were routinely achieving marks of 80 per cent and above? Rather than having some students achieve only 40 per cent by only half-grasping all of the curriculum, might it not be more satisfactory to identify 40 per cent of existing material that everyone graduating from the particular degree course would be expected to know?

The model I offer is called '4, 3, 2, 1' because it is based on the idea of considering four elements of a degree course, each requiring specific methods, representing proportions of credit in the ratios shown in Table 4.1. The approach does not de-emphasize content in favour of content-less procedures, but rather it identifies elements of a degree course that can perhaps be most effectively addressed by specific procedures.

Table 4.1 Elements of the 4, 3, 2, 1 model

Element of study	Percentage credit	Proportion
Core	40	4
Contextual and professional	30	3
Independent	20	2
Reflective and cultural	10	1
Total	100	10

Core study
In a science or engineering course, it should be possible to arrive at a judgement of what every graduate should know in order to be deemed a chemist or a civil engineer or whatever. Such material could be taught by self-paced study procedures (see pages 52–4) designed to ensure mastery of the material for all students.

Contextual and professional study
For engineers, such studies are all those concerned with problem-solving and project management. They might include all the knowledge and skills necessary for competent professional practice, such as management science, accountancy and finance, modern languages, group-work and communication skills, and familiarity with the political, social and economic constraints on the design of physical systems. For scientists, such studies are those concerned with the design, management and execution of complex experiments.

Problem-based procedures, which seem to be effective in medical education (see Barrows and Tamblyn, 1980; Neufeld and Chong, 1984), could be extensively used in this component of the degree. Cawley (1989) reports work of this kind in engineering. Most laboratory work would probably fit into this category (though see below), and any experience students could be given off-campus during term-time or out-of-term could be drawn upon to help students to see the core material through the lens of professional concerns. Much of the literature on learning from experience is helpful in this area (see, for example, Hendel and Enright, 1978; Yelon and Duley, 1978; Conrad and Hedin, 1982b; Duley, 1982; Evans, 1987; see also Chapter 3 above).

Independent study
To capitalize on the research-orientation of universities, and to offer scope for high-flying students, guided independent study similar to that pioneered at the University of East London (see Chapter 3) could be used in this component of the course. Likewise, undergraduate research opportunities (to be covered in Chapter 6) could give highly motivated and competent students the chance to assist the academic staff with their researches –

whether or not individual project work (which is usual in degree courses) were to be considered as part of this component.

Reflective and cultural studies

In Chapter 3, I have argued the case for an element of reflexivity, or cultural migration, to be considered as part of *every* degree course. For science and engineering courses, my view is that this can best be achieved by offering studies in the humanities which allow students to sustain interests developed before university, but more importantly give them familiarity with modes of academic discourse outside their main disciplines – specifically those that may help them to see the 'normal' concerns of their disciplines from a questioning perspective.

With very considerable differences between students in terms of their pre-university schooling (not necessarily in their ability, which may not have been revealed by their achievement), it is becoming increasingly difficult to 'target' first-year courses so that all students will have a good experience of learning. One attraction of a mastery approach for core material is that it helps students to 'find their own level'; but perhaps more importantly, a mastery approach allows universities to determine precisely what a student should know in order to achieve the pass mark. The elements of independent study can offer very valuable evidence concerning the capabilities of very gifted students. In short, the overall design attempts to offer diversity in approach, and to link this diversity systematically to the perceived objects of a degree course.

For other types of course, it might be possible to turn the model inside-out: making 10 per cent of the course core material, 20 per cent single-discipline study, 30 per cent theme-based (i.e. drawing on several disciplines to explore common themes) and 40 per cent options in cognate areas. Whatever design is adopted, my hope would be that an appropriate overall balance would be sought between the dimensions of theory and practice, society and the individual.

Again, I would hope that every student could be given an opportunity to do work as part of the degree course that was of direct benefit to other people. Like undergraduate research opportunities, study service can not only provide the focus for students in linking theory and practice, and their perceptions of self and of society, it can also be a fruitful link between the learning needs of the students and the researches of the academic staff. It is to research, therefore, that I now turn.

5

Research

The three major questions about research paid for out of tax-payers' funds are: What should be done? Who should do it? Where should it be done? This chapter will argue that the emphasis in universities should be on research in which students can assist; that every academic should be encouraged to undertake at least scholarship, the foundation on which research is based (although the division of labour within departments may result in some doing more research, and spending more time on scholarship, than others); and that funds for research should in principle be available to any university, albeit with selectivity. To make best possible use of facilities, the maximum flexibility of movement of individuals across institutional boundaries should be encouraged – so that individuals can identify with functions without being unduly inhibited by the institutional arrangements whereby functions are distributed.

There is an abundant literature on performance indicators in research, particularly on research in science and technology (for example, Andrews, 1979; OECD, 1984; Cozzens *et al.*, 1989). This chapter, however, concentrates on ends rather than means.

Issues

So powerfully organized, and in many subjects so well-established, are fields of research that it may seem sheer lunacy to attempt to discuss research in general as a topic within a treatise on the nature of university education. However, with funds for research inevitably limited (whether or not the supply at present in particular countries is appropriate), it is highly desirable that those with control of funds should have some principle of selection.

There is, in principle, literally no limit to what we might wish to know – and, in consequence, to what we might wish to spend on getting that knowledge. Some questions, like those concerning the size and nature of the universe, are of such staggering imaginative fascination that even societies, like the United Kingdom, which are deficient in providing many of the necessities of life (adequate health care, provision for old people, proper schooling for all children, an efficient transport network etc.) nevertheless vote public money for work on them. Other questions, in anthropology, sociology, archaeology, history etc., concerning who we are, where we came from and where we may be going, are equally fascinating. How do we decide which to support? Just as there can be no logical way of choosing between moral systems, so there can be no logical way of choosing between fields of enquiry. The question, therefore, resolves itself into *who* decides just as much as on *how* they decide.

There are also pragmatic questions which are being discussed with some urgency in the United Kingdom. Should all university teachers do research? Are research and teaching detachable functions? Should some universities cease to be research centres? Does the 'quality' of an institution depend upon the research 'productivity' of its staff?

The element of liberal humanist thought (derived from existentialist thinking) concerned with making choices as a fundamental aspect of being human necessarily implies a preference for diffusing the points of choice and decision as widely as possible through society. The larger the number of persons who can take part in decisions, the more liberal will a society be. Rather than having decisions between research areas made by a small group of wise persons (who could not conceivably have any basis of deciding between fields other than their own opinions, or prejudices), the object to be sought is of spreading decision-making as widely as possible through society.

To decide research objectives by plebiscite would be an obvious nonsense. However, one way of earthing decisions about the objectives of research and fruitful social process is to link funding for *some* research to the teaching done by universities. In this way, the pattern of demand for courses (a crude but credible indicator of what people find sufficiently interesting to merit an investment of their lives) can act as a social regulator of research priorities. Interestingly, the less the investment of personal time can be seen as a *financial* investment (as differentials between the earnings of graduates and the earnings of non-graduates narrow), the more reliable does demand for courses become as an indicator of a society's purely intellectual interests.

It is extremely important to note my use of the word *some*: it is neither possible nor desirable for all research to be undertaken in universities. More money is already spent by industry on research for its own purposes on its own premises than by government on research in universities. Moreover, much publicly funded research, particularly in science and technology, is defence related, and carried out in research establishments and/or in industry.

The distinction between types of research is not only one of 'pure' and 'applied'. Much 'applied' research (such as that on semi-conducting materials) requires work on basic and fundamental natural phenomena. The phrase 'strategic research' is commonly used for this type of work. The principle of selection concerning who should do what research and where requires an additional factor.

Central to the thesis of this book has been the proposition that criticism

of the work of universities must proceed on primarily moral grounds because universities are concerned (in ways which are less true of other institutions that nevertheless include education of some sort among their
functions) with the nourishment of persons. Universities are, from this
perspective, very special types of institution embodying in some ways a
society's image of itself. If universities continue to be foci of research activities as well as of teaching, there should be at least the possibility of ensuring
a distribution of research effort which reflects the full range of questions
and issues people think important. Such a proposal does not, of course,
imply any inhibition (other than a diminished share of public funding) on
any individual or group in a university doing any research deemed interesting or important; rather, it offers a method of ensuring (within the limits
of what can be set aside for the life of the mind) a liberal allocation of
effort between different types of institution.

The research to be done in universities should be primarily research in
which students (postgraduate if not undergraduate) can in principle take
part – because, I have argued, the basic *raison d'être* of universities is the
nourishment of persons. The research agenda of universities, nationally if
not separately by institution, should reflect a balance of interests similar to
that of the curriculum. Students already value those parts of the curriculum
that most closely reflect the research interests of the academic staff, namely
final-year projects.

It would be crass to propose that all research in universities should at all
times and in all details be absorbed with maintaining the balance between
theory and practice, society and individual that is the defining characteristic
of liberal humanism: if research is to be efficient and effective, specialization
is necessary and desirable. The balance of concerns, can, perhaps, best be
assured at the points of input to and output from a programme of research.

Those who vote funds for research have a controlling influence at the
point of input. The process of selection for funding of research to be done
in universities might usefully include questions such as these:

- Does the research proposal promise advance in theory (or understanding
  of basic processes) as well as the mere accumulation of information?
- Does it also contain some indication of how the theory (ideas) involved
  relate to practice, to the resolution (directly or indirectly) of issues concerned with the apparatus of living?
- Are the interests of some discernible section of society likely to be nourished by the fruits of the research?
- Are the ideas and theories likely to be valuable, or are specific findings likely
  to be intelligible and useful, to people outside the educating institution?
- Does the research promise an enlargement in any way of our perception
  of what it means to be a person? Do the likely outcomes (theoretical or
  practical) promise to stretch our imaginations?
- Will the procedures of research to be adopted or the findings hoped for
  nourish in any way the *teaching* function of the university?

- Will it be possible, for example, for postgraduate students to take part in or extend the research proposed?
- Will there be opportunities for undergraduate research?
- Will the research help other educating institutions too?

At the point of output, those who publish the fruits of research – and indirectly those who purchase the publications which contain those fruits – have a great responsibility, not only because academics at present survive through their productivity in publication, but also because publications translate colleges with walls into colleges without walls.

One of the most remarkable phenomena of the present century has been the colossal growth in the number of academic journals and in the number of papers published in them. One baleful consequence is that the very word 'academic' has come to be used in popular parlance for the arcane and useless. What is to be done? The tide cannot easily be stopped: within academic disciplines, within the narrow confines of each academic sub-discipline, each paper has, no doubt its honoured place. What we need to ensure is that vehicles for the publication of research exist in the middle ground between the super-specialized journals of particular research interests and the popular journals which can make their way by public sales. In short, there may be merit in devising methods for the subsidy of forms of publication (in print and in other modes) designed to give access to the wider, tax-paying public to the work undertaken in universities.

What we currently lack is a way of talking to each other. We will make no progress in achieving effective communication until people are able and willing to 'locate' their research in a context of ideas that is meaningful to people not in their special disciplines. The Royal Society, through its Committee on the Public Understanding of Science (COPUS), has already taken important steps in this regard, in, for example, sponsoring an annual prize for the best book popularizing science. The very process of popularization demands that new ideas are given context.

The matter is not as complex as it may sound. One of the most rewarding things that I do is to offer workshops on technical presentation to professional scientists and engineers from universities, industry and commerce, and the civil service who have to present very complex technical information to audiences ranging from their professional peers, through funding bodies, to graduate and undergraduate students. With the exception of a few ideas in advanced mathematics and in theoretical physics, I have never come across a piece of research that cannot, with due thought, be made intelligible, interesting and accessible to non-specialists. The sustaining framework of ideas that makes new material intelligible to non-specialists can be developed by numerous strategies; elsewhere (Goodlad, 1990b) I have outlined eighteen strategies by which scientists and engineers can make their ideas interesting and intelligible to other people. What is common to all of the strategies is for speakers to offer to their listeners the courtesy of trying to identify, and identify with, their listeners' *reasons* for wanting to involve themselves with the subject. (Similar principles, of course, apply to written technical communication.)

The question of how to talk about a subject intelligibly to non-specialists inevitably, and fruitfully, raises the basic question of what the given piece of research is *for*. No research is ever really 'blue sky' in the sense of having *no* end in view. 'Pure' research is nearly always devoted to understanding some fundamental process in nature, the root of some intriguing idea, the mode of impact of a work of literature. If the researcher can give no coherent account of what he or she is trying to do, the research is probably confused – or pointless.

In this regard, F. L. Lucas, writing in *The Search for Good Sense*, has words which might well be read by any young person embarking upon a period of university research, and by his or her intended supervisor:

> It seems to me, then, mere common sense never to undertake a piece of work, or read a book, without asking 'is it worth the amount of life it will cost?'; never to pursue any kind of knowledge (apart from practical necessities) without demanding 'will it make life more vivid, more intelligent, more complete, more real?' Then one at least has some principle to simplify existence, instead of emulating La Fontaine's dogs who, seeing an appetising dead mule afloat offshore, tried drinking up the sea to get it – and burst.
>
> It is said that the Emperor Tiberius used to tease scholars by asking them abstruse and futile questions such as the name of Hecuba's mother. (She was, it appears, the dimmest of dim creatures, called Metope.) What was Hecuba to him? Nothing, except an occasion for pedantry. It would doubtless have been suicidal for the scholars to retort to that irritable potentate, 'what does Hecuba's mother matter?' yet it is important, I think, to keep asking oneself precisely that question, alike in life and in learning. For the learned world is overpopulated with Hecuba's mothers. Nine PhD dissertations in ten are written about her. Her children are Legion; and most of them abortive. It is fatal to get wedded to her; she is both phantom and vampire.
>
> (Lucas, 1961: 19–20)

If *balance*, rather than Hecuba's mother, were to be sought more often, the word 'academic' might begin to shed its pejorative associations.

Heresies

The health of the research of the university is controlled, *inter alia*, by the intellectual fertility of the researchers, the beneficence of funding agencies and the willingness of publishers to disseminate the findings of the research. Some of the heresies listed below, and located in Figure 5.1, are prone to be committed variously by funding agencies as much as by universities or university people.

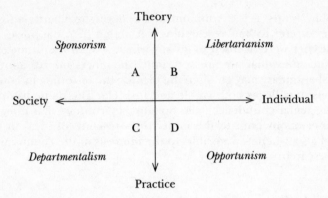

Figure 5.1 The heresies of research.

Heresy 9: Sponsorism (A)

Distortion of the notion of accountability into the over-prescription and control by government or other funding agencies of the form and content of research to the detriment of individual insight, creativity, even eccentricity.

Line-item budgets which require specification of how each penny will be spent and how each minute of time will be used are death to collegial research. If research is to have an educative function, there must be time for people to throw ideas around, to talk to each other. In Martin Trow's vivid words: 'There have got to be lots of rocks for little furry creatures to hide in!' The heresy of sponsorism occurs whenever the element of trust, a fundamental component of the liberal humanist respect for persons, becomes lost in overly tidy bureaucratic procedures.

Another danger, bemoaned by Robert Nisbet (1971) as part of 'the degradation of the academic dogma', is what he calls 'the higher capitalism', the undue influence over the direction of academic research by liaisons with industrial organizations. In principle, there is no reason why strategic research alliances should not foster research that is fruitful in nourishing simultaneously both practice and theory; in reality, as Webster (1994) demonstrates, alliances with sponsors can produce 'torquing' of a research agenda that may not be in harmony with the purposes of universities. Certainly if sponsors put limits on the freedom of publication of universities, one of the distinctive features of universities is in danger of being subverted.

Heresy 10: Libertarianism (B)

Trivial or irresponsible research carried out in the name of 'academic freedom'.

If academics are to avoid the rigidities of other people's heresy of sponsorism, it follows that they must act responsibly. Where funds for research come from public funds, it is a symptom of the heresy of libertarianism for an academic to refer to 'my' research as if it were a personal possession, as if the researcher were licensed to go any which way. In the balance between society and individual, we are very much members one of another. The individual antiquary may go where he pleases; the historian, by contrast, has obligations to colleges both visible and invisible. The naturalist may 'accumulate in genial confidence'; the botanist, by contrast, has obligations to relate observations both to the underlying structure of ideas in the discipline and also, whenever possible, to the interests of the community paying for the research.

Heresy 11: Departmentalism (C)

Intellectual territoriality, or the desire simply to keep a team together, as misleading motives for research.

In the quadrant concerned with the social and the practical (C) lurk the temptations for the researcher to plan work and seek funds without regard to interests wider than those of the immediate sub-discipline, or for the misguidedly 'humanitarian' motive of 'keeping a team together'. If the team's work is effectively finished, then the team should disband. This implies, of course, that the university as a whole should take some responsibility for the support of its members. The tendency for academic appointments to become *de facto* the property of departments (even of sections within departments) has diminished during the current period of financial stringency; it should not be allowed to return.

It may be convenient to the administration of a university to devolve responsibility for appointments to research sections (indeed, the principle of disseminating points of decision-making to facilitate choice seems to require this). But academics take their identity in large part from their research: that is why research sections which nourish this sense of identity have become what Becher and Kogan (1980: 79) call basic units. It is also why academic disputes can be so bitter: an attack on a person's ideas can be perceived as an attack on the person.

If research units or sections are not subject to collegial control, the entire cultural life of a university may become frozen. Departmentalism could have been listed as a heresy under curriculum, teaching methods or college organization. It is placed firmly in this section (under research) because identity of intellectual interest (nourished by research) is at the root of much social organization in academic organizations. Anyone who doubts this should read *Academic Tribes and Territories* (1991) by Tony Becher! In this regard, does one perhaps detect a cloud no larger than a man's hand in the setting up in universities in recent years of interdisciplinary research centres (IRCs)? Necessary as they may be for drawing researchers together from a variety of disciplines into fields that have some strategic significance, there is the awkward question of what will happen if and when their research is finished. Paradoxically, the answer may be in *strengthening*, rather than loosening, the ties of the researchers with their home departments – provided that the home departments themselves represent an institutional commitment to some enduring questions of fundamental intellectual and social interest.

Heresy 12: Opportunism (D)

This heresy is present when the search for 'truth' gives way to the search for 'international visibility', pursuit of big money and/or contracts.

In the competition for research funds, no one would survive long who did not exercise initiative, imagination, resourcefulness and a certain entrepreneurialism in getting research funding. Such energy only becomes heresy when the other motives for research become lost to sight.

Preferences

Rationale

In the preceding paragraphs, no distinction has been made between research, scholarship and reflection. This is no accident. Although there are obvious differences between them, the differences are much less important than the similarities. Research (the testing of hypotheses against evidence) and scholarship (the refinement of observation) have in common the search for truth, or (to avoid that wearisome cliché) the search for order. Perhaps this is why, in the prestige pecking order of academic pursuits, those activities have highest prestige which provide the maximum of explanatory power with the minimum of concepts: fundamental particle physics, mathematics, philosophy.

'All art', said Walter Pater, 'constantly aspires towards the condition of music.' All academic research, it might be observed, aspires towards a cosmic reductionism in which all things become intelligible from a single perspective. That the quest is endless (and the goal, in the last analysis, incapable of achievement) makes it no less exciting. What it is crucial to note is that the inspiration for research is (if not in a theological, then in a secular, sense) transcendent. Why climb Everest? 'Because it is there.' The answer is one of pure mysticism. The rationale for much research is, ultimately, mystical, but the researcher, unlike the mystic, is almost certainly supported by public funds. It seems not unreasonable, then, to ask for some justification of research – even if the final statement is a mystical one.

It would be crass indeed to expect that every piece of research be justified line-by-line in terms of social utility, or, for that matter, in terms of any of the principles that in dynamic tension sustain the position advanced in this book. However, one of the important reasons for maintaining research in universities is that the invitation to offer a rationale is, in principle, always present. This, indeed, is one of the reasons why it is fruitful for research and teaching to be done by the same persons. Most researchers know that they sort out their ideas very effectively not only by explaining them at research conferences, but also by trying to explain them simply to students.

The interwoven rhythm of teaching and research gives opportunity for ideas to 'simmer on the back burner' – opportunity, in short, for periods of diversion from the routine and rush of research to allow ideas to flow. What can be immensely stimulating is to let the 'simmering' take place while one is rehearsing the fundamental issues of a discipline with students. Hearing about what is going on at the research frontier can be a significant stimulus to students, a strengthening of their morale as they cope with the demands of getting there.

If *undergraduate* research opportunities, in addition to *graduate* research opportunities, can be provided, researchers are likely to find the stimulus of explaining the rationale of their work to eager young would-be assistants extremely invigorating (see McVicar and MacGavern, 1984; and see Chapter 6 below).

Some sort of collegial context seems desirable for many types of research – with the opportunity for researchers to share ideas with other people. If this collegiality is sought in the institutional context most centrally involved with the liberal humanist project, i.e. the university, the 'location' of research within a sufficiently wide framework will be assured.

Funding strategies to permit reflection

It is often more difficult to work out the rationale for research, to interpret and communicate the significance of one's studies, than it is to carry out the 'busy-work' of literature searching, questionnaire design, fact-gathering, number-crunching and so forth. With the twin pressures of teaching more students per unit of resource and of hunting for 'funny money' (the operating expenses of research), many academics are showing signs of manifest harassment. Perhaps, with the sheer competitiveness of most universities nowadays, this is to be expected. It is, however, inimical to any sort of collegial perspective on research. What can be done?

First, it is essential for bodies concerned with awarding research funds to build into research contracts funds specifically to permit and encourage reflection. A realistic element of 'overheads' is one way in which this can be achieved, with the award-winning institution being given freedom of action in deciding how to deploy such overheads. Likewise, they could earmark funds for literature reviews designed specifically to point up the significance of what has been discovered. Some educational research projects have provision for 'dissemination' as a funded activity with very much this aim in mind. I am well aware that the strategy I am advocating might lead to *less* research being undertaken and/or to research being done by fewer people. But I believe that such a strategy would lead to a more balanced disposition of funds, and perhaps a more considered diffusion of research ideas.

Second, the policy of dual-funding, currently under debate in the United Kingdom, is an indispensable aid to reflection. While academics may not unreasonably expect to have to compete for 'funny money', the ecology of academic departments depends crucially on some departmental money being allocated for research. Not all academics in a department will have the desire or capacity to do research; but all benefit by being in contact with those who do the research. The academic who has taken on the burden of being admissions tutor, or senior tutor (departmental trouble shooters), or administrator of examinations, may not be able to do as much research as other members of a department. But the administrator-academic is likely to be kept fresh and up-to-date by departmental colloquia, coffee-room discussions and so forth while shouldering burdens which allow other people to do the basic formative work. Likewise, academics who take on higher-than-average teaching loads can nourish and be nourished by a burden-sharing arrangement of this sort. Their very presence does also act as a spur to the researchers – who may realize that if they do not carry the flag, they may have to carry the stretchers!

Third, the ecology of departments sketched above does have one great danger: that of type-casting. It may be indispensable for individuals to have the opportunity to uncouple from time to time from large administrative burdens, or even from the demands of keeping up research productivity. Sabbatical leave (alas, almost unknown in some universities and increasingly perceived as a luxury in most) is of crucial importance. Funding strategies, for teaching, administration and research, should, if possible, accommodate sabbatical leave.

Fourth, it is not self-evident that departmental research strength should be rewarded with more support, research weakness with less. Trow (1994: 23–4) has reported how at the University of California, Berkeley, the discovery of serious deficiencies in the research quality of some of its departments of biology in the early 1980s led to a major study and reform of the organization of biology at the university that involved major investments in both buildings and people. The distribution of funds for research is a matter that requires constant review, with clearly articulated principles.

It may, however, be a more limited (and therefore more realistic) goal to seek to stimulate research, and the diffusion of research ideas, by exchanges of personnel and/or by promoting and encouraging the greater permeability of institutional boundaries.

Permeability of institutional boundaries

In which institutions should research take place? In a way, to put the question thus starkly is to present a false picture (like the question 'have you stopped beating your wife?'). The issue becomes clearer if one asks instead: how can each individual in a university (teacher or student) be put into direct contact with the advancing edge of learning?

What is increasingly apparent with processes of selectivity being much in vogue is that a concentration of scarce resources into specific places is seen by government as highly desirable on purely economic grounds: libraries holding long runs of expensive periodicals or expensive books; well-found laboratories with complex equipment; computerized data archives; and so forth. What is equally obvious, if the liberal humanist project that I am advocating is to be sustained, is that individual academics in higher education institutions need to be as fully absorbed in theory and practice, society and individual enlightenment as possible. If *institutions* are to specialize (for economic and other reasons), *individuals* must at least have the opportunity to move freely between institutional contexts in which these are best realized.

The process of short-term or interwoven secondment may be important for this purpose. Becher (1994: 69) has commended secondments as a way of fostering interdisciplinary dialogues in higher education. During his researches into disciplinary subcultures, he discovered interesting examples of individuals who had migrated across disciplinary boundaries: a chemist who had migrated to biology, an anthropologist in a history department, a plant pathologist who had made a new career studying fish vision and a literature specialist who had switched from sixteenth-century poetry to modern drama. Describing this process as the intellectual counterpart of easier travel between countries, Becher commends the potential value of outside observers seeing, describing and sharing in the disciplinary domains of others. *Within* disciplines, the process of secondment of individuals from one sector of higher education to another, or between higher education and commerce or government, is already well-established. It needs to be encouraged.

What would be grossly anti-humanist would be to define institutional boundaries too rigidly and thereby to deny individuals the possibility of movement between them. (It would also, I suspect, be both inefficient and ineffective in terms of research productivity.) This is where the distinction made in Chapter 1 between institutions, functions and individuals is absolutely fundamental. Institutional specialization may be highly desirable – with some universities becoming 'centres of excellence' in particular types of research and others becoming, perhaps, centres of excellence in consultancy or in teaching. Without some arrangement for the movement of people between institutions, there is a danger of some institutions (by implication the people who work in them) being permanently written down as second- or third-class.

These matters take us to issues of college organization which are addressed in Chapter 6.

6

College Organization

College organization is of crucial importance in the liberal humanist approach to higher education. Institutions, which constitute the embodiment of ideas and ideals, are themselves vehicles for statements of educational theory – not only through their prospectuses, charters or other symbolic or formal statements of intention but also through their day-to-day actions and, indeed, their buildings.

Issues

The polarities of theory–practice and society–individual (see Figure 6.1) are as valuable for criticism of college organization as for criticism of curriculum, teaching methods and research agenda. The theory–practice axis in the context of college organization concerns the nature of 'college' as a distinct social institution, a theoretical entity as it were, distinct from and yet compounded of the various elements of practice necessary for academic activity to take place. The issue here is one of whether 'college culture', as a sub-culture within the wider society, is a desirable or harmful phenomenon.

It is, of course, possible for similar courses of study to be offered in different environments; for example, a school sixth form or a tertiary (FE) college. King (1976), for example, has explored how different environments affect the individual's experience of being a student. In higher education, too, tastes and fashions may vary. Some years ago Haymarket Publications changed the title of its annual volume *Which University?* to *Which Degree?* Does this imply that students nowadays seek courses rather than communities? Which is to be preferred: academic communities which make some sort of demands on the total personalities (identities) of students, or servicing organizations which meet intellectual needs alone?

Perhaps the distinction can be highlighted by the following ideal type distinction (see Goodlad, 1983a) between 'airport culture' and 'monastic culture'. (An ideal type is, of course, Weber's term for a sociological approximation which aids description and analysis. It does not imply approval of the social form examined.) One can draw parallels between the institutional characteristics

Table 6.1 'Airport' and 'monastic' cultures compared

Airport	Monastery
1. Place of transit	1. Place of permanent membership
2. Relationships severely functional	2. Relationships valued for their own sake
3. No interest of institution in the social lives of people passing through it	3. Paternalistic interest in social (and spiritual) development of individuals
4. No discipline except for technical infringements of the law	4. Strong sense of 'appropriate' behaviour, disciplining of deviants
5. Cafeteria catering	5. *Table d'hôte* dining central to life of institution
6. Entertainment an extension of outside culture: *Playboy, New Yorker* etc., films, TV	6. Own entertainment
7. Centrality duty-free store, drugs to narcotize	7. Centrality of chapel to reinforce sense of shared identity and commitment
(*Gesellschaft*)	(*Gemeinschaft*)

of institutions of higher education and, respectively, airports and monasteries (see Table 6.1). As indicated in Table 6.1, some of these features approximate loosely to the *Gesellschaft* and *Gemeinschaft* of Tonnies (1957): they appear in college cultures, which may be contrasted as in Table 6.2.

This sketch, like most ideal types, is a gross over-simplification. Oxbridge colleges, which at one time or another and variously have exhibited all the characteristics listed under monastic culture, are changing their institutional arrangements towards the convenience and functional comforts of airport culture. My own college, King's College, Cambridge, for example, now has cafeteria catering – even electronic games in the JCR. Likewise, as Jacqueline Scherer (1972) discovered over twenty years ago, various types of communal living emerge in airport culture colleges. More recently, Ruth Finnegan (1994) has given a vivid account of how sophisticated information technology is giving rise to forms of electronic community among staff and students of the Open University. Despite these intermediate cases, the ideal types do represent two quite distinct cultural forms, each of which has advantages and disadvantages.

'Monastic' institutions, for example, particularly if small and culturally segregated (or perhaps physically isolated), can become narrow, socially limited and oppressive. Some American universities, for example, ban fraternities on their campuses because of their tendency to become socially, politically or ethnically exclusive. Their advocates, however, would claim

Table 6.2 'Airport' and 'monastic' aspects of college cultures

Airport culture: non-collegiate	Monastic culture: collegiate
1. Place of transit. Students have to register each year. No significant rites of passage.	1. Permanent membership. Students matriculate and are then college members for ever. Obituaries in college journal, entire graduating class invited to college every ten years.
2. Relationships functional. Students admitted if 'ticket' is in order. (contest mobility)	2. Relationships partly for their own sake. Students admitted if manifestly e.g. 'a Kingsman' even with poor (or no) A levels. (sponsored mobility)*
3. No interest of institution in the social lives of its members. Relationships of staff and students formal and remote.	3. Paternalistic interest of institution in its members. Students invited to dinner with their tutors. No female visitors to college after midnight. 'Exeats' needed for absence from the university.
4. No discipline – except for that of the law. 'Double punishment' an issue raised by student union if institution seeks to impose its own sanctions on students who break civil law.	4. Strong sense of appropriate behaviour; students sent down or 'rusticated' for disgracing the college.
5. Cafeteria catering. Pay-as-you-eat.	5. Communal dining. Students pay for a term's dinners. Whole college dines at the same time if physically possible.
6. Entertainment an extension of the 'outside world'. Union sponsors 'pop' concerts. Union bookshop – textbooks and paperbacks only. Pinball machines in halls of residence. Much TV watching.	6. Own entertainment. College choir or orchestra. Intimate revue. Even the manifestly incompetent expected to make up a team for inter-collegiate sports if necessary.
7. Centrality of the union bar as a focus of any social activity that may exist.	7. Centrality of library or chapel: foundation scholars may be required to attend chapel on certain formal occasions.
8. Characteristic complaint *anomie* – dealt with by the new maternalism of student counsellors, psychiatrists etc.	8. Characteristic complaint *alienation* – dealt with by high-spirited rebellion against oppressive rules. Mythology of mischief climbing into college over spiked railings, escape from proctors and 'bulldogs' etc.

* The contrast between contest and sponsored mobility is that of Turner (1961).

that fraternities offer an all-involving collegiate experience which is of benefit to the individual, although the rites of passage of fraternity life (see Leemon, 1972) might strike many as almost totalitarian in their reduction of the individuality of the person.

In 'airport culture' institutions, by contrast, there may be a lack of ceremonies which (to use a Durkheimian phrase) put the community into action, multiply relationships between people and signify, in some public way, the values held to be important. These ceremonies need not, of course, be grand ritual occasions (degree ceremonies and so forth), but rather occasions when staff and students meet to express some common purpose: for example, colloquia by final-year students; seminars with visiting speakers; rites of passage, welcoming of new staff or students, farewells to graduates or retiring staff, inaugural lectures by new professors; small college or departmental celebrations to mark the publication of a book or the winning of a prize or outside honour. Such modest occasions indicate that people are valued (if only one-dimensionally in their academic persona); they are, as it were, 'pre-institutional' manifestations which, if sustained, multiplied, formalized, centrally organized or centrally focused, become 'monastic'.

Once again, liberal humanism seeks a balance. The isolated individual is inconceivable. We express a large part of ourselves through our relationships with one another. Even Robinson Crusoe's self-sufficiency is only noteworthy because it symbolizes technical substitution for the division of labour in society. Morally responsible action only has meaning when individuals make choices which recognize the effect each person's action has on the lives of other people. However, the negation of individual action by group pressure (psychological or physical) is the fuel of pogroms, witch-hunts and totalitarianism of all forms.

Likewise, on the theory–practice axis, everything that turns individual learning into education (curriculum, teaching methods, research aimed at achieving consensus knowledge) implies the organizing presence of social institutions. The 'college' must have some claim on our social selves. If we do not greet colleagues through our necessary collegial transactions as three-dimensional persons, we are guilty at best of discourtesy, at worst of barbarism. Yet to centre one's life wholly on the 'college' is to risk losing touch with the wider society in which practice draws strength from that sense of personal identity, *esprit de corps* and maturity which collegiality should nourish.

Heresies

Once again, the heresies in the area of college organization as in other areas represent deviations from the position of balance (see Figure 6.1).

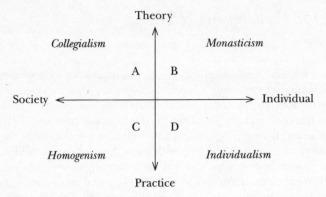

Figure 6.1 The heresies of college organization.

Heresy 13: Collegialism (A)

Submersion of the individual in the collegiate either by misguided pressure from peers or by personal choice.

Rites of passage, such as departmental coming-up dinners (freshers' dinners), are a legitimate part of the identity-forming ritual of a collegiate institution. They drift into heresy when they involve, for example, the systematic humiliation of freshmen – 'hazing' in American usage. At another level, students who never leave the campus may suffer from 'campus neurosis', a danger which is greatest in isolated or 'green-field' campuses, or where a university dominates a town, or where transport is poor, though often found in colleges in big cities, where students may be lonely. Symptoms of 'campus neurosis' are persistent complaints about college catering, or continuous grizzling about minor and trivial aspects of social arrangements.

Members of the academic staff drifting into the heresy of collegialism begin to show all the symptoms of being institutionalized, i.e. inability to see themselves in any dimension or in any role in society except that associated with their collegial role.

Heresy 14: Monasticism (B)

Withdrawal of the 'college' from the 'world' or self-isolation of sub-cultures within higher education institutions.

Interestingly, monasticism is a heresy as likely to flourish in 'airport culture' institutions as in 'monastic' ones: such are the anomic stresses of large institutions that like-minded individuals gather for psychic protection. One particular student society (athletic, recreational, social) may become the sole identity-giving agency for an individual. Similarly, the small research section (or sub-department) may become the main social, as well as intellectual, base of the member of staff.

Heresy 15: Homogenism (C)

No attempt to separate the 'college' from the 'world'.

Any form of social institution offers opportunities for conviviality, for the deeply humanizing rejoicing of people in one another's company. To deny the opportunities (in factory, office, church or any form of social institution) is to miss the richest possibilities of a liberally humane society. To do so in education, through becoming interested in persons only through the most narrowly specialized concern with some tiny aspect of their formation, is to slide into a heresy which is not only morally reprehensible, but also technically inefficient. Some gathering together of people for 'serendipitous mutuality' seems to be a necessary complement to, for example, distance learning (by whose technical ingenuities it might seem possible to educate people without extracting them at all from the wider society). The Open University, for example, has found summer schools and local counsellors indispensable.

Heresy 16: Individualism (D)

Separation of the individual from the collegiate.

Clark Kerr's (1963) definition of a university as a set of individual faculty entrepreneurs united only by a common grievance over parking amusingly describes this heresy. If total immersion of the staff in the affairs of the 'college' is a sign of being institutionalized, using the college merely as a parking lot or mailing address is equally damaging. Likewise, for students to be 'brown baggers' (commuting to college as if to a factory or office) is to miss many of the possibilities which college offers.

Some sort of deliberate exposure to the collegiate seems sensible. Once again, one cannot prove that this is so: Chickering's massive study, *Commuting Versus Resident Students* (1974), of over 169,000 students in the United States (about 10 per cent of the total student population of the USA at the time) suffers from the same difficulties as 'impact' studies (see Chapter 2): it is technically impossible to get around the problem that much of the eventual difference between commuting and residential students may depend more on the interests, motivation, prior social characteristics, selection of style of life, selection by their college for a certain type of residence etc. than on any effect of the residential experience itself. The fact that place of residence varied according to socio-economic status (fraternity students typically being from the highest status families, followed by students in dormitories or halls of residence, then by those in rooming houses and finally by those living at home (see Chickering, 1974: 45)), should itself alert us to this possibility.

Preferences

One must beware of the phoney or paternalistic! This book is an approach – not a prescription. Its style is to argue and persuade rather than to suggest force, because choices freely entered into represent a more profound commitment by the individual person than ones constrained by pressures. The preferences below reflect this approach.

Size of institution

The notion of a person being advanced in this book can be nourished or crushed by the type of institution in which persons express their fundamental ideas about both academic work and other matters. Because many higher education institutions (medical schools, for example) are currently having to contemplate forms of association with other institutions, it is timely to examine the relevant considerations.

Economists have argued (see Sear, 1983) that financial economies increase more or less indefinitely with every increase in the size of institutions of higher education. By contrast, some sociologists and psychologists suggest that very large institutions may have a damaging effect on the morale and motivation of individuals who may perceive themselves to be socially redundant. For example, Thomas and Chickering (1983: 45) have suggested that individuals in very large educating institutions experience 'redundancy'. Six general consequences are associated with this:

(a) A smaller proportion of the 'inhabitants' actively participate;

(b) The activities and responsibilities of those who do participate become less varied and more specialised;

(c) Persons with marginal ability are left out, ignored, and actively denied opportunities to participate;

(d) Evaluation of performance shifts from how well a person's abilities actually fit the requirements for participation, for a given position, or for an area of responsibility, to how good one person is compared to another; in educational terms, evaluation shifts from criterion referenced evaluation to norm referenced evaluation. Furthermore, as numbers increase and put pressure on the need to discriminate, judgements are made on the basis of increasingly fine distinctions;

(e) A hierarchy of prestige and power develops;

(f) Rules for conduct, definitions of appropriate behaviours, standards for performance, become increasingly formalized and rigid.

All of these factors have effects on students' sense of involvement with their colleges and, Thomas and Chickering suggest, on their efficiency and effectiveness in studying. Their catalogue might suggest that small institutions were to be universally preferred to large ones. There is, however, an extremely important distinction which Martin Trow (1983) makes: that between the nominal and effective size of an institution.

The life of an educating institution is not a unitary phenomenon: one can redefine institutional boundaries according to the functions with which one is concerned at any given time. Trow observes that within the University of California, Berkeley, for example, it is possible, depending on what one is trying to do at any one time, to be a member of a seminar group of three; a research group of ten; a department of fifty; a lecture class of 900; a campus of 29,000; a state university system of 120,000 (with, for example, credit transfer rights between campuses, a common computerized library catalogue system etc.). As if that were not enough, there is a sharing of library facilities between Berkeley and Stanford University (which is fifty miles away). A library card to the Berkeley library is also honoured at Stanford. It is no matter that the University of California is a 'public' (state) university and that Stanford is a 'private' one; in respect of circulation they function almost as one library.

Thus a college may be part of a university which organizes some central facilities (libraries, personnel and accountancy, mainframe computing or computer networking, student health services, careers advice and student counselling units etc.) which it would be uneconomic for smaller units to run for themselves. Within a college, likewise, departments and sections may perform efficiently functions which it would be uneconomic for other units (either larger or smaller) to perform. Schumacher (1983: 64) demonstrates this point by offering an analytic diagram illustrating economies and diseconomies of scale at various levels of educational organization. In short, given appropriate planning, both students and staff can enjoy the collegial benefits of small institutions and the academic advantages of big ones. (Oxford and Cambridge, of course, developed the idea about 500 years ago; Gaff (1969) describes more recent experiments in the United States to replicate the pattern.)

Nowadays, it is the research section rather than the college that may offer the identity-giving element of university life. Becher's researches (1991) on the power of disciplinary groupings, and the earlier researches of Becher and Kogan (1980) on the resilience of 'basic units' within the organization of higher education, support this notion. If American experience is anything to go by, the huge expansion of numbers in the United Kingdom higher education system within the past decade will probably be accompanied by increasing differentiation of function between institutions. Already, as Halsey (1992) has shown in his book *The Decline of Donnish Dominion*, and as has also been shown by Tapper and Salter (1992) in their book *Oxford, Cambridge and the Changing Idea of the University*, Oxford and Cambridge have changed their functions somewhat and are emerging as the leading research institutions. Whether or not all universities in the United Kingdom can or should attempt to emulate them is a matter for debate.

Forms of association between academic institutions
The feeling of personal worth, adequacy and fulfilment of persons is a

crucial part of the equation whenever economies of scale are being contemplated for educating institutions. The identity and visibility of institutions of relatively small scale can contribute to this. As mergers of institutions continue to be on the agenda of educational planners, it is important to keep this perception in mind.

To illustrate some of the issues, I will offer as a case study some observations on the development over the past twenty-five years of a number of church colleges of education, which in the period when 'rationalization' was most fashionable (1970 to about 1987) were in danger of being 'tidied away' by over-zealous civil servants, but which now represent a distinctive sector of higher education currently (1994) educating over 65,000 undergraduate and postgraduate students – more students, in fact, than were present in all the universities in Great Britain immediately after the Second World War.

Most of these colleges owe their existence to developments in the United Kingdom at the beginning of the nineteenth century in the training of intending teachers. Special institutions were established by the British and Foreign School Society at Borough Road College and the National Society based on a training school near Gray's Inn. The 1840s saw the establishment of many Anglican colleges; Roman Catholic colleges were first founded in the 1850s. Later in the century, colleges were founded by the Congregationalists and Methodists. Not only did these colleges establish teacher training in the United Kingdom, they also offered the possibility for students to take BA and BSc degrees outside the universities.

State teacher training colleges attached to universities were set up after the Cross Commission in 1890, and by 1900 about a third of all teachers were being trained in these colleges. Colleges were founded by the local authorities in the early years of the twentieth century. By 1969, there were 107 LEA colleges of education and fifty-one voluntary colleges of education: twenty-seven Anglican, fifteen Roman Catholic, three British and Foreign School Society, two Methodist and four so-called 'Unitary' colleges (Westhill (Free Church), Homerton, Froebel, and Goldsmith's).

Since 1972, there has been a drastic reduction in the number of free-standing voluntary colleges in England. Today, only nineteen remain (full details of the many closures and mergers may be found in Locke *et al.*, 1985). Having been delivering higher education for over 120 years, the remaining voluntary colleges represent a long and distinguished history of service to the nation – and, of interest in this book, a distinctive ethos for the maintenance of which appropriate administrative shapes continue to be sought. In the pursuit of these, the colleges have contemplated various types of collaboration with which to achieve the best balance between nominal and effective size.

Forms of collaboration between voluntary colleges and other academic institutions
Several types of association have been undertaken between voluntary colleges and other institutions, including the following.

1. *Cooperation*: loose association, involving a sharing of resources, but not necessarily a common academic programme.
2. *Association*: Close association for purposes of academic planning between two or more similar, autonomous colleges (like that pursued until recently between Newman and Westhill colleges in Birmingham).
3. *Federation*, with an over-arching council but with the retention of separate governing bodies (such as that at the Roehampton Institute); apparently only legally possible between independent institutions of similar corporate status.
4. *Integration* (as between the colleges of St Paul and St Mary in Cheltenham, now part of the Cheltenham and Gloucester College of Higher Education), involving the uniting of two voluntary institutions of similar size (and preferably of the same denominational affiliation) to form a single larger entity.
5. *Incorporation* (as at Derbyshire College of Higher Education, now Derbyshire University, which incorporated Bishop Lonsdale College of Education), by the setting up of a single governing body.
6. *Absorption* of one institution by another, involving the buy-out of the smaller by the larger institution (as in the absorption of St Luke's College, Exeter, by Exeter University).

Since the demise of the Council for National Academic Awards, which validated the degrees of many of the voluntary colleges, most voluntary colleges have entered into association with universities, which started with the validation of their degree programmes but is now moving fruitfully, in many cases, towards accreditation which secures a greater degree of autonomy for the voluntary colleges. (The Cheltenham and Gloucester College of Higher Education, which has over 7,000 students, awards its own first degrees, and provides facilities for doctorates under the aegis of Bristol University.)

The issue of collaboration between a voluntary college and another higher education institution only becomes contentious when the governors of the voluntary college (and/or its providing body) believe the college's independent identity to be in danger of being compromised. Similar concerns will arise whenever any other type of higher education institution seeks common cause with another one to achieve economies of scale, greater political 'crunch' or higher visibility on the higher education scene. The following matters seem to be critical.

(1) *Clarity of purpose*. In his influential study of three famous American liberal arts colleges (*The Distinctive College: Antioch, Reed, and Swarthmore*), Burton Clark (1970) identifies the existence of a strong unifying idea (or 'saga') as crucial to a college (see also Clark, 1972, 1979). Such an idea does not mean that a college is strikingly different from other colleges (though it may be), but rather that it (meaning its governors, staff and students) has a vision of what the college intends to do, and does do, very, very well. This vision can then be communicated to the wider public upon

whom the college relies not only for recruitment but also for political support and funding.

The voluntary colleges, through the religious nature of their foundation, undoubtedly have such ideas (see Skinner, 1968; Wyatt, 1977a, b; Gay, 1978; VSCC, 1985; McGregor, 1991). Clark's researches suggest that such ideas are not just sentimental accretions, but are powerful integrating forces with consequences for effective college management. Later commentators have made similar observations; for example, Dill (1982: 319) urges that, given the distinctive nature of academic organization, the maintenance of the expressive aspects of academic community deserves much more attention than it has received in discussions of academic management. Similarly, Chaffee (1984), examining successful strategic management in a sample of small private colleges in the USA, suggests that presidents who base their actions on symbolic as well as substantive concerns will be more effective leaders than those who are not conscious of symbolic implications.

The problems that occur in federations result mainly from clashes of purpose, expressed often in disputes over areas of jurisdiction.

(2) *Clarity about areas of jurisdiction.* Higher education institutions forming links with others need to be very clear in mind about areas of jurisdiction. For example, voluntary colleges, particularly those with religious providing bodies, have experienced a tension between the academic and the collegiate. Effective academic organization nowadays seems to require strong *departments*, with concentration of academic staff onto specific sites; effective *college* organization may seem to require retention of control over functions which technical requirements suggest should become the responsibility of whatever over-arching body constitutes or represents the federation.

Difficult though it may be, it is desirable that institutions joining a federation or forming some other such type of association should retain some influence over the selection and employment of staff, the selection of students, curriculum and teaching methods, and the agenda of research and development. Where academic posts are supported from public funds, secular concerns must necessarily prevail. But if an institution gets a reputation for a certain type of 'saga', there will be an element of self-selection among those seeking admission. Again, with public funds for research and development being harder than ever to secure, opportunities become proportionately stronger for colleges to sponsor initiatives with private funds that are in harmony with their objects.

(3) *The crucial role of presidents or principals.* The role of a college in a federation is similar to that of a ship in a fleet; it does not lose its identity, but rather becomes the more effective through joint action. To pursue the analogy, a ship's company has an identity largely independent of the particular vessel which the captain and crew operate. The point of the analogy is to stress that, like a ship's company, a 'college' can have a life of its own, independent of its ownership of or identification with specific buildings – useful though buildings may be in giving outward and visible shape to inward and spiritual ideas.

Perhaps more congenial to church colleges is the analogy of a church or religious order. A church in a locality is the body of Christian people, not a specific building – although the church congregation may meet in and operate from a specific building. Likewise, a religious order has a 'collegial' existence almost entirely unrelated to specific property. Indeed, the *Concise Oxford Dictionary* definition of 'college' is 'organized body of persons with shared functions and privileges'. This important concept of a 'college without walls' is recognized in many complex, as well as in many significant minor, ways. For example, the annual report of King's College Cambridge may record that there are 5,800 members of the college 'of whom 600 are in residence'.

It is in nourishing, sustaining and expressing the loyalty-evoking 'saga' that the principal or president has a key role, although (see Kerr and Gade, 1986) it is only one of many roles. For a religiously based institution, the task is that of holding all aspects of a college's life together within the framework of a religious tradition rather than that of being an expert in a particular academic specialism (although a principal may be this too).

Collegiality, the sense of holding a common purpose, is often regarded as one of the defining characteristics of voluntary colleges. It does not, however, result entirely from the accident of relative smallness of institutional size, which is not, and was not, a unique characteristic; Carswell (1985), for example, has reminded us how very small were most pre-war universities in the United Kingdom. Rather, collegiality is the product of deliberate and sustained effort which may be aided by, but is not necessarily *caused* by, smallness of size. This point is well illustrated by Roberts (1994), who describes how the sense of a learning community was achieved as one church college (Chester) more than doubled in size.

Nor is the principal's influence on collegiality the only one. Much of the collegiality of the four constituent colleges of the Imperial College of Science, Technology and Medicine (The City & Guilds College, The Royal College of Science, The Royal School of Mines, and St Mary's Hospital Medical School) is sustained by the alumni organizations which operate an international network of contacts, and by the constituent college unions within Imperial College which nourish students' sense of collective identity by social activities, many of which have an almost ritual quality – serving, like the elementary forms of the religious life studied by Emile Durkheim, no very visible purpose other than that of putting the group into action. Rag collections, sporting fixtures, mascot raids, dinners, debates, dances and so forth provide a rich texture of social life which crosses departmental boundaries, and exists in addition to the more specialized social and recreational clubs and societies for which the wider entity of the Imperial College Union is required – orchestras and choirs, drama, mountaineering, gliding and suchlike clubs.

Colleges with a religious tradition have an even greater range of possibilities to draw upon, and an educated sensibility to the rhythms of social life by which communities define themselves. Some of these rhythms reflect those of the Christian year, so that religious festivals can be the occasion for special college functions, and the rhythm of the academic life can be creatively punctuated by events reminding students of the Christian way of life (such as, for example, the suspension of some classes on Ascension Day).

The celebration of community, as anthropologists remind us (e.g. Douglas, 1966), depends to a great extent on the signification of boundaries. Rites of passage typically celebrate the movement of individuals from one social state to another. There are abundant opportunities in the secular life of colleges (quite apart from those interwoven with the religious life) for colleges to recognize transitions: arrivals and departures of students; beginnings and endings of terms; inaugural lectures by newly appointed staff. Even routine meetings, particularly if accompanied by the sharing of food ('the breaking of bread'), can assume a profound conviviality in Polanyi's (1958) sense of the word.

So complex is the articulation of the symbolic life of an academic community that it rightly requires the attention of a principal. In the University of Oxford, college heads are not allowed to hold chairs. This modest rule recognizes that although an individual may hold a position in the faculty simultaneously with a senior college post, the two are functionally independent.

As many voluntary colleges move into some type of affiliation to universities, it will be important to sustain the independent visibility of the colleges. The above sketch of the role of the principal does not reduce it to that of hall warden (an idea that would be rightly resisted). Nor does the analysis of collegiality reduce the role to that of mere social lubrication. For colleges with a religious foundation, principals could continue to be chosen primarily by providing bodies and college governors partly for the visibility in, and contribution to, the life and work of the church constituencies that the foundations represent. The work of the principals of such colleges is indeed one form of contribution to the life and work of the church. This work is concerned with mediation between academic and religious ways of life and thought, just as the roles of presidents of large secular universities may be concerned with mediation between the university world and the worlds of finance, industry and politics.

Mechanisms of mutuality

In striving for balance between theory and practice (college and world), society and individual, it is desirable to seek activities which accord as closely as possible with what people see to be central to the common purpose upon which they have embarked. That is to say, contrived 'collegiality' is less desirable than spontaneous collegiality, or, to use a phrase of Elizabeth Templeton, 'energy directed towards a common goal'. A good example of this type of academically focused collegiality is the MIT undergraduate research opportunities programme (see MacVicar and McGavern, 1984) mentioned in Chapter 3.

Conceived originally as 'pastoral' measures, to give MIT students a greater sense of belonging in an institution famous above all for its research, arrangements were made for undergraduates to work alongside members of the academic staff in their research laboratories. Students were not given 'student projects' (of the sort already widespread in undergraduate curricula) but were, rather, co-opted as research assistants – sometimes paid, sometimes rewarded with academic credit, often rewarded by the sheer satisfaction of being involved at the frontiers of knowledge. Experience has shown that undergraduate research activities of this sort not only give students a genuine experience of collegiality (by letting them become members of lively cells within the larger organization), but also fulfil the fundamental aims of the curriculum through a teaching method which is congenial to both academic staff and students.

Students in the Imperial College Undergraduate Research Opportunities Programme (UROP), which is modelled on that at MIT, were interviewed in depth in 1989 and 1990 about their experiences of UROP work (see Goodlad, 1992). In 1991, and again in 1992, students who had done UROP work during the academic year and/or summer vacation were sent questionnaires containing statements based upon the comments that their predecessors had made: they were asked to rate the statements on a five-point scale according to the extent to which they felt that the items had been achieved for them personally. With maximum possible ratings of 100, a number of the items that were most highly valued by 1992 respondents ($n = 33$) are listed below (1991 scores, $n = 44$, in parentheses after the 1992 ratings):

- I enjoyed the independence I was given working, 88 (84);
- I enjoyed being given responsibility in my UROP work, 85 (85);
- I valued the chance to talk with the postgraduate (PG) students and the post-docs/research assistants, 79 (70);
- through UROP work, I learned the importance of planning work, 79 (70);
- I felt accepted as a co-worker with the staff and PGs, 82 (78);
- my UROP work was intellectually stimulating, 76 (79).

Furthermore, the activities in which the students took part represent, by definition, precisely that type of research urged in Chapter 5 as the most desirable: research in which students can take part.

It may be objected that undergraduate research opportunities are all very well for MIT or Imperial College, which have massive research activities and highly selected students: what about other types of institution? What can they do? Undergraduate research is, in fact, only a contemporary variant of the ancient *atelier* or studio principle in which pupil works alongside master, watching, listening, helping, gradually acquiring understanding and control, until ready to take responsibility for more and more of the work. There are abundant opportunities at every level of most applied subjects for the rediscovery of this approach.

As already urged (in Chapter 4), engagement–reflection modes of study (including study service) have considerable pedagogic attractions. They are also attractive as offering mechanisms of mutuality because in most cases staff and students work alongside each other. That they link theory and practice, social responsiveness and the nourishment of individual capabilities as well, makes them even more attractive.

Meeting the needs of part-time students

Facilitation rather than control has been an underlying theme of this book – the liberating of the student within the curriculum, removal of obstacles to learning through appropriate teaching methods, releasing of the educative possibilities of research by prudent selection of topics. Facilitation is also desirable as an administrative ideal.

For stimulating collegial experiences within non-collegial organizations, relaxed, imaginative and flexible administration is crucial. Every grouping of individuals within an institution of higher education is, in potential, a miniature college, a focus for intellectual, and thus social, transaction. Often, however, the transience of the student population and the absorption of the staff with research can lead to missed opportunities. Small gestures of (what the Americans call) 'administrative facilitation' can work wonders in helping students to create collegial cells within larger 'airport culture' organizations: access to duplicating equipment, use of rooms out of hours, use of catering equipment (tea urns, cups, plates etc.); assistance with typing letters; someone to take incoming telephone messages. The approach is not one of academic staff telling students what to do (or, for that matter, of doing 'it' for them); it is, rather, the positive disposition to others which sees the full range of their needs as persons.

One notable feature of the development of higher education in recent years has been the looser coupling between students and their institutions, considerable migration across national borders (through such schemes as ERASMUS and SOCRATES), the massive growth in distance learning techniques, credit transfer and 'franchising' of courses from universities to colleges of further education. With the level of the student grant being progressively reduced, many students are also having to work during term-time as well as during vacations so that, although they are nominally 'full-time', they are effectively part-time.

Although some institutions may continue to aim their provision primarily at 18–22-year-olds of relatively homogeneous achievement at entry, most universities have already experienced a growth in the numbers of adult or mature students, many of whom prefer or need (for domestic or professional reasons) to study part-time. The needs of these students has been receiving significant attention (see for example, Woodley *et al.*, 1987; NIACE, 1989; Smith and Saunders, 1991; Tight, 1991). Many of these students will be more demanding of universities than younger students; they will approach what is offered as customers rather than as supplicants. Indeed, Tight (1991) sees positive advantages for *all* students flowing from what he describes as a 'part-time perspective' in terms of alternative models of the provision of higher education affecting entry requirements, study patterns, study location, accreditation, course content, teaching–learning methods, assessment, costs and fees.

If the increase in the numbers of adult and/or part-time students forces attention on to the needs of students (rather than perhaps the convenience of we who teach), that, from the perspective of this book, will be welcome.

A few years ago, during a visit to Phoenix, Arizona, I learned of a phenomenon known there as 'the swirl'. In common with other states in the USA, Arizona permits and encourages students to achieve credits in the community college system that they can then 'cash' at the University of Arizona. Many students do this because it is often easier to use a community college near to one's home or work for part-time study. The sophisticated information technology of the community colleges' registration system had picked up that many students were registering at several community colleges simultaneously – picking up some credits, for example, at sunrise seminars in college A, going on to a job, and picking up additional credits from a sunset seminar at college B. One consequence of this 'swirl' of eager students around the system was that car parking provision, which had originally been estimated at one space for every two student lecture-room seats, had had to be revised upward to one car parking space for *every* lecture-room seat. In a city 150 miles across, there seems to be space for this at which we in the United Kingdom can only gaze in awe. But the experience of Phoenix, in a massively market-driven situation, does point up a thought that we in the United Kingdom must also ponder. If, to adapt Clark Kerr's (1963) *obiter dictum*, we do not want a university to become a grouping of faculty and *student* entrepreneurs united only by a common grievance over parking, we will need to take more seriously than we have perhaps done to date the business of giving adult and/or part time students a valid and worthwhile experience of college as a place with a visible and tangible ethos.

7

From Student to System

Although the independent, autonomous scholar may always have been a sustaining myth rather than a sociological reality, there has undoubtedly been a growing perception in many countries that higher education has been moving 'from autonomy to systems', to use the title of a collection of essays by James Perkins (1972). The colossal cost of higher education has been part of the political agenda ever since the state became involved in meeting some of it. However, influential though the state may be, it is not necessarily the main player (or stakeholder to use contemporary jargon). In *The Higher Education System*, his wide-ranging study of the ways in which higher education is organized in different countries, Burton Clark (1983) uses a triangle to illustrate the dynamic tension between those at its corners: students, professors and the state. He suggests that there is a progressive movement of systems towards the middle of the triangle. For example, the Swedish system has moved away from significant state control whereas the United States, often thought of as the main 'free market' model, has moved towards large-scale state systems. The United Kingdom has, in his analysis, moved from domination by the professorate much more towards the middle of the triangle – although it sometimes feels as though we have one giant university controlled by the state through funding councils that have data on every individual academic!

It might be thought that a book with the nourishment of persons as its central concern would be politically disposed towards students as those who should exercise greatest control. This would be to over-simplify. The Christian-compatible framework that I have sketched is part of a tradition, in MacIntyre's sense of the word, in which *all* spheres of human activity are held in scope, and in which there is continuing and continuous debate about the economic, political and social measures that will maintain fidelity to the notion of persons at its core.

My main assertion has been that we cannot talk intelligibly about the nature and purpose of universities without some vision of what sort of persons will emerge from them. This is not the same as a demand for uniformity. Institutions will locate themselves at different points of the theory–practice, society–individual axes: specializing in one or more of the segments indicated in Figure 2.1. My own institution, the Imperial College of Science, Technology and Medicine, is probably best seen as having a bias towards theory; most of its research, even when apparently 'applied,' is concerned with measurement, bringing to bear on specific problems ideas drawn from fundamental science, and using the problems in turn to test the validity of the theory. Other institutions (perhaps some of the '1992 universities', the former polytechnics) may locate themselves more clearly in the applied domain, undertaking research and development work very closely related to the presenting problems of industry, and offering degree courses that are a more direct preparation for a specific occupation than those of Imperial College. To judge them all by the same indicators of performance is manifest nonsense. 'First destination of employment' measures may be inappropriate for institutions preparing students for jobs that have not yet been invented, just as research council income (rather than consultancy and/or contract research income) might be an inappropriate indicator for others.

Wherever institutions locate themselves through their 'mission statements,' my assertion would be that they would do well to avoid the heresies I have sketched! I will certainly not appear, like the characters of *Monty Python's Flying Circus*, leaping off a London bus clad in red robes and cackling gleefully that 'Nobody ever expects the Spanish Inquisition!' However, having given this book the sub-title of *Sixteen Forms of Heresy in Higher Education*, I am resigned to the fact that the points that follow may be labelled 'Goodlad's inquisition'. In anticipation of this, I have used the phrase in the next sub-heading!

Goodlad's inquisition

For heuristic purposes, the previous chapters have separated out matters that in practice are experienced in an all-at-once manner: it is now time to put them back together again.

Teaching methods must reflect in detail the nature of the subject matter in the curriculum. In universities, the curriculum, particularly at the level of third-year and fourth-year options, of individual projects and essays, and of group projects, is in a constant ferment fuelled by the research interests of the academic staff. All of these functions of curriculum formation, research and teaching go on in an institutional setting which can significantly influence the personal and professional development of all who work there. The interconnections are as important as the ideas.

Although the previous chapters have listed a number of my personal preferences for activity that is consonant with the basic moral perspective I am advocating, my main concern is *with the perspective itself*. It is a concern that I think many colleagues share and that others might find acceptable whether or not they share the cultural presuppositions that underlie the tradition. Accordingly, in the suggestions that follow, I address myself to a fellow university teacher – confident that the necessary refocusing can readily be undertaken by readers who may be putative students, their teachers, their parents or those who control or bear the costs of their education.

If you, my colleague, warm to the 'doctrine of man' I have put forward, and if you accept my assertion that universities are specialized institutions that reflect in significant ways the intellectual core of modern culture, you will no doubt have your own set of preferences. To help you to sharpen these up, I offer in this concluding section a checklist of key issues spanning the domains of curriculum, teaching methods, research and college organization, and drawing upon the arguments advanced in the book.

For the sake of simplicity, I have phrased the checklist assuming that you are a university teacher responsible for part of a degree programme, and that you wish to put on paper material that will help your students with your course. If, however, you are a student, or a planner, or a funder, or a quality-assessment *aficionado*, please make the necessary adjustment.

- Do your materials indicate the overall aim, purpose and plan of your section of the degree programme?
- Are explicit links made with your students' previous work and/or academic studies, with parallel parts of the degree programme, with the theoretical concerns of your discipline and with any practical applications of the idea?
- Have you used every available opportunity to encourage engagement–reflection modes of study in your students – through problem-based learning, project work, opportunities for students to assist with your researches, opportunities for study service etc.? Are these activities systematically keyed in to the core of your curriculum in ways that illuminate both theory and practice, and that stimulate debate about how your students relate to the wider society?
- Have you indicated how and why your course has its specific orientation – so that your students can see how it relates to your fundamental concerns, and theirs?
- Have you given enough information for your students to commit themselves fully to your course and yet have the freedom to take part in other valuable activities? For example, are the details about individual teaching sessions adequate for students to judge the amount of preparatory or follow-up work to do? Are the dates, times and places of each teaching activity listed, and are precise details of coursework submissions (*deadlines, format*) and examinations spelled out?
- Do the detailed objectives of each activity reflect appropriately your overall aim and purpose?
- Are your objectives clear of fuzzy words that leave students in uncertainty (*know, understand, appreciate, have a good grasp of* etc.) and strong in precise words that specify what they should be able to do (*identify, name, describe, order, construct, list, evaluate, state, distinguish, specify, design* etc.)?

- Have you provided specific opportunities for your students to discuss with you the 'whys and wherefores' of your course, and is there adequate opportunity for them to contribute *their own* ideas through essays, projects, seminar discussions etc.?
- If some of your students missed (through illness or accident) some of your classes (particularly the ones early in the course), would they know how to find their way around the material: what to read (*full publication details*), where to go (*rooms, buildings*), what to do (*registration, safety procedures, CAL instructions* etc.), how to prepare for assessment (*notes on essay writing, project management* etc.)?
- If your subject lends itself to such treatment, do you offer PSI (personalized systems of instruction) modules to enable students to take more control of their own learning?
- Are the modes of assessment you use reliable and precise? Whether they are or not, you might do students the courtesy of inviting them to set up criteria of their own, and assess their own and one another's work using their criteria and yours.
- Do the modes of assessment actually assess the knowledge, skills and attitudes that you wish to promote? You may wish, in addition to listing logistic details of dates, deadlines, etc., to show in your materials what your assessment techniques are designed to test: *examinations, closed-book or open-book; reports; oral presentations; practical tests; viva voce tests* etc.
- Have you taken steps to ensure that your students are not overloaded with work or harassed by assessment regimes? Again, you may wish to explain to your students *how* you approached this problem.
- In addition to the above, how have you tried to ensure that your students adopt deep, rather than surface or strategic, approaches to their studying?
- Have you taken every opportunity to explain your research to other people – in particular, students (graduate or undergraduate) who may in due course help with it and members of the public who (through their taxes) may be paying for it?
- If your institution is rich in research facilities, are you active in ensuring that they are made available as far as feasible to colleagues from less well-endowed universities? Or if you work in one of the less well-endowed institutions, have you examined every possibility of collaborative work with colleagues in geographically reachable institutions with better facilities than your own?
- If yours is an 'airport culture' institution, how do you and your colleagues give students a sense of belonging? Is every opportunity for conviviality seized upon (*rites of passage, colloquia, project presentations, field-trip parties* etc.)?
- If yours is a 'monastic culture' institution, do you take steps to extend the range of your own and your students' social and intellectual experience? For example, if you are a member of a tight-knit research section, do you and your colleagues make a point of going to a number of research presentations by groups in other (cognate) fields?

- If yours is a very large institution (whether or not it feels like an airport), have you and your colleagues evolved ways of establishing effective sub-units for the social and intellectual development of yourselves and your students?
- If yours is a very small institution ('monastic' or otherwise), have you and your colleagues built links with individuals and groups in other institutions large or small that extend your range of contacts? (Your 'effective' size could in this way become larger than your 'nominal' size.)
- Can your department, section or college offer 'administrative facilitation' (properly accounted for and paid for) to help into action pre-institutional groupings of staff and students?

As no unique definition of quality is ever likely to be found meaningful, none of these matters may be deemed *sufficient*. However, I would argue that they are all *necessary* if we are to avoid doing things that manifestly *lack* quality. So subject yourself from time to time to this friendly inquisition, and you will, I trust, avoid slipping into any of the sixteen forms of heresy in higher education. You will also, I confidently predict, achieve a personal view of what 'quality' means, the better to resist any more threatening inquisition our masters may invent.

Finally, if we focus on the student and constantly debate how the system aids or impedes our concerns, we should find a way that leads without difficulty from student to system.

Appendix: The Sixteen Forms of Heresy

The heresies of curriculum

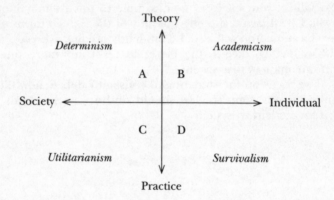

Heresy 1: Determinism (A)

Belief in the exclusively social genesis of knowledge and over-statement of the (often undeniable) class interest in knowledge.

Heresy 2: Academicism (B)

Reification of knowledge, found whenever disciplines are defined as though they were somehow independent of the people who created them.

Heresy 3: Utilitarianism (C)

The adaptationist tendency to see learning always as a means to some social end, concerned with 'practice', never as a source of personal enlightenment, revelation and/or satisfaction to the individual.

Heresy 4: Survivalism (D)

The over-emphasis on education as supplying job skills.

The heresies of teaching methods

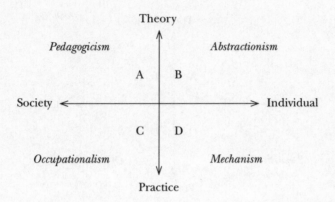

Heresy 5: Pedagogicism (A)

Over-planning of education, or over-dependence on some theory of learning, to the extent that the provisional and tentative nature of educational theory is lost to sight.

Heresy 6: Abstractionism (B)

Over-emphasis on systems of thought, concepts, intellectual structures, to the neglect of the contextual details which alone can give them meaning.

Heresy 7: Occupationalism (C)

Over-emphasis on the practical 'needs of society' (or industry) or the 'demands of the discipline' in specifying the types of learning to be undertaken.

Heresy 8: Mechanism (D)

The vice of treating persons as part of some system or organization, neglecting other dimensions of their personality.

The heresies of research

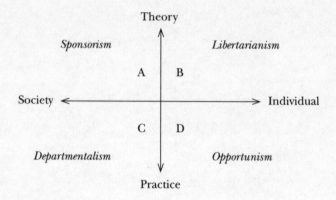

Heresy 9: Sponsorism (A)

Distortion of the notion of accountability into the over-prescription and control by government or other funding agencies of the form and content of research to the detriment of individual insight, creativity, even eccentricity.

Heresy 10: Libertarianism (B)

Trivial or irresponsible research carried out in the name of 'academic freedom'.

Heresy 11: Departmentalism (C)

Intellectual territoriality, or the desire simply to keep a team together, as misleading motives for research.

Heresy 12: Opportunism (D)

This heresy is present when the search for 'truth' gives way to the search for 'international visibility', pursuit of big money and/or contracts.

The heresies of college organization

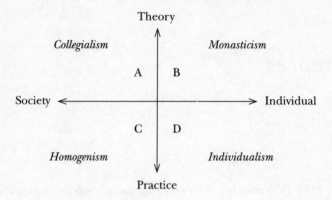

Heresy 13: Collegialism (A)

Submersion of the individual in the collegiate, either by misguided pressure from peers or by personal choice.

Heresy 14: Monasticism (B)

Withdrawal of the 'college' from the 'world' or self-isolation of sub-cultures within higher education institutions.

Heresy 15: Homogenism (C)

No attempt to separate the 'college' from the 'world'.

Heresy 16: Individualism (D)

Separation of the individual from the collegiate.

References

ACTION (1978) *Evaluating Service-learning Programs: a Guide for Program Coordinators.* Washington, DC: National Center for Service Learning.

ACTION (1979) *The Service-learning Educator: a Guide for Program Management.* Washington, DC: National Center for Service Learning.

Aiello, N.C. and Wolfle, L.M. (1980) A meta-analysis of individualized instruction in science. Paper presented at the annual meeting of the American Educational Research Association. Boston, MA: 7–11 April 1980.

Andrews, F.M. (ed.) (1979) *Scientific Productivity: the Effectiveness of Research Groups in Six Countries.* Cambridge: Cambridge University Press and UNESCO.

Annan, N. (1963) The universities, *Encounter,* April.

Argyris, C. (1982) *Reasoning, Learning and Action.* San Francisco: Jossey-Bass.

Astin, A.W. (1977) *Four Critical Years: Effects of College on Beliefs, Attitudes and Knowledge.* San Francisco: Jossey-Bass.

Atkin, J.M. (1987) Review of five HMI reports on initial teacher training institutions. *Studies in Higher Education,* 12(2): 229–32.

Bailey, F.G. (1977) *Morality and Expediency: the Folklore of Academic Politics.* Oxford: Basil Blackwell.

Ball, C. (1985) What the hell is quality?, in D. Urwin (ed.) *Fitness for Purpose, Essays in Higher Education by C. Ball.* Guildford: SRHE and NFER-Nelson.

Banton, M. (1965) *Roles: an Introduction to the Study of Social Relations.* London: Tavistock.

Barnett, C. (1986) *The Audit of War: the Illusion and Reality of Britain as a Great Nation.* London: Macmillan.

Barnett, R. (1990) *The Idea of Higher Education.* Buckingham: SRHE and Open University Press.

Barnett, R. (1992) *Improving Higher Education: Total Quality Care.* Buckingham: SRHE and Open University Press.

Barnett, R., Parry, G., Cox, R., Loder, C. and Williams, G. (1994) *Assessment of the Quality of Higher Education: a Review and an Evaluation.* Report for the Higher Education Funding Councils for England and Wales by the Centre for Higher Education Studies, Institute of Education, University of London.

Barrows, H.S. and Tamblyn, R. (1980) *Problem-based Learning: an Approach to Medical Education.* New York: Springer.

Becher, T. (1991) *Academic Tribes and Territories.* Milton Keynes: SRHE and Open University Press.

Becher, T. (1994) Interdisciplinarity and community, in R. Barnett (ed.) *Academic Community: Discourse or Discord?* London: Jessica Kingsley.

Becher, T. and Kogan, M. (1980) *Process and Structure in Higher Education*. London: Heinemann.

Bees, M. and Swords, M. (1990) *National Vocational Qualifications and Further Education*. London: Kogan Page in association with the National Council of Vocational Qualifications.

Bird, C. (1975) *The Case Against College*. New York: David McKay.

Bloom, B.S. (1956) *Taxonomy of Educational Objectives. Handbook 1: Cognitive Domain*. New York: David McKay.

Bok, S.X. (1982) *Beyond the Ivory Tower*. Cambridge, MA: Harvard University Press.

Boot, R. and Reynolds, M. (1983) *Learning and Experience in Formal Education*. Manchester: Manchester University Department of Adult Education.

Boud, D. (ed.) (1985) *Problem-based Learning in Education for the Professions*. Sydney: Higher Education Research and Development Society of Australia.

Boud, D., Keogh, R. and Walker, D. (eds) (1985) *Reflection: Turning Experience into Learning*. London: Kogan Page.

Bourdieu, P. and Passeron, J.-C. (1977) *Reproduction in Education, Society and Culture*. London: Sage.

Bowles, S. and Gintis, H. (1976) *Schooling in Capitalist America*. New York: Basic Books.

Boydell, T. (1976) *Experiential Learning*. Manchester: University of Manchester Department of Adult Education.

Boys, C.J., Brennan, J., Henkel, M., Kirkland, J., Kogan, M. and Youll, P.J. (1988) *Higher Education and the Preparation for Work*. London: Jessica Kingsley.

Brancher, D.M. (1975) Projects in the development of general education, *European Journal of Engineering Education*, 1(1): 35–40.

Brennan, J. and McGeevor, P. (1988) *Graduates at Work: Degree Courses and the Labour Market*. London: Jessica Kingsley.

Bridge, W. and Elton, L.R.B. (1977) *Higher Education Learning Project (Physics)*. London: Nuffield Foundation.

Brooks, S.E. and Althof, J.E. (1979) *Enriching the Liberal Arts through Experiential Learning*. London: Jossey-Bass.

Brown, J. and Goodlad, S. (1971) Grassroots engineering, *Electronics and Power*, February: 49–53.

Bruner, J.S. (1977) *The Process of Education*. London: Harvard University Press.

Button, B.L., Sims, R. and White, L. (1990) Experience of proctoring over three years at Nottingham Polytechnic, in S. Goodlad and B. Hirst (eds) *Explorations in Peer Tutoring*. Oxford: Basil Blackwell.

CAEL (1975a) *The Learning and Assessment of Personal Skills: Guidelines for Administrators and Faculty*, CAEL working paper 4. Princeton, NJ: Cooperative Assessment of Experiential Learning.

CAEL (1975b) *The Learning and Assessment of Interpersonal Skills: Guidelines for Students*, CAEL working paper 5. Princeton, NJ: Cooperative Assessment of Experiential Learning.

CAEL (1975c) *A Guide for Assessing Prior Experience through Portfolios*, CAEL working paper 6. Princeton, NJ: Cooperative Assessment of Experiential Learning.

CAEL (1975d) *A Student Handbook on Preparing a Portfolio for the Assessment of Prior Experiential Learning*, CAEL working paper 7. Princeton, NJ: Cooperative Assessment of Experiential Learning.

CAEL (1975e) *A Task-based Model for Assessing Work Experience*, CAEL working paper 8. Princeton, NJ: Cooperative Assessment of Experiential Learning.

CAEL (1975f) *A Student Guide to Learning through College-sponsored Work Experience*, CAEL working paper 9. Princeton, NJ: Cooperative Assessment of Experiential Learning.

Carswell, J. (1985) *Government and the Universities 1960–1980.* Cambridge: Cambridge University Press.

Cave, M., Hanney, S., Kogan, M. and Trevett, G. (1988) *The Use of Performance Indicators in Higher Education.* London: Jessica Kingsley.

Cawley, P. (1989) The introduction of a problem-based option into a conventional engineering degree course, *Studies in Higher Education*, 14(1): 83–95.

Chaffee, E.E. (1984) Successful strategic management in small private colleges, *Journal of Higher Education*, 55(22): 212–41.

Chickering, A.W. (1969) *Education and Identity.* San Francisco: Jossey-Bass.

Chickering, A.W. (1974) *Commuting versus Resident Students.* San Francisco: Jossey-Bass.

Chickering, A.W. (1977) *Experience and Learning: an Introduction to Experiential Learning.* New Rochelle, NY: Change Magazine Press.

Clark, B. (1970) *The Distinctive College: Antioch, Reed and Swarthmore.* Chicago: Aldine.

Clark, B. (1972) The organizational saga in higher education, *Administrative Science Quarterly*, 17: 178–84.

Clark, B. (1979) The many pathways of academic co-ordination, *Higher Education*, 8(3): 251–67.

Clark, B. (1983) *The Higher Education System.* Berkeley, University of California Press.

Conrad, D. and Hedin, D. (eds) (1982a) *Youth Participation and Experiential Education.* New York: The Haworth Press.

Conrad, D. and Hedin, D. (eds) (1982b) *Experiential Education Evaluation Project.* St Paul: University of Minnesota.

Cozzens, S.E., Healey, P., Rip, A. and Ziman, J. (eds) (1989) *The Research System in Transition.* London: Kluwer Academic.

Craft, A. (ed.) (1992) *Quality Assurance in Higher Education.* London: Falmer Press.

Daiches, D. (ed.) (1964) *The Idea of a New University: an Experiment in Sussex.* London: Andre Deutsch.

Dainton Committee (1968) *Enquiry into the Flow of Candidates in Science and Technology into Higher Education.* Council for Scientific Policy, Department of Education and Science. The Dainton Report, Cmnd 3541. London: HMSO.

Daly, D.W. and Robertson, S.M. (eds) (1978) *Keller Plan in the Classroom.* Glasgow: Scottish Council for Educational Technology.

Davis, R.H., Duley, J.S. and Alexander, L.T. (1977) *Field Experience: Guides for the Improvement of Instruction in Higher Education.* East Lansing: Michigan State University Instructional Media Center.

de Rudder, H. (1994) The quality issue in German higher education, *European Journal of Education*, 29(2): 201–19.

Dewey, J. (1963) *Experience and Education.* New York: Collier.

Dill, D.D. (1982) The management of academic culture: notes on the management of meaning and social integration, *Higher Education*, 11: 303–20.

Douglas, M. (1966) *Purity and Danger.* London: Routledge and Kegan Paul.

Doyle, R.J. and Chickering, A.W. (1982) Crediting service learning, in S. Goodlad (ed.) *Study Service: an Examination of Community Service as a Method of Study in Higher Education.* Windsor: NFER-Nelson.

Duley, J. (1978) *Basic Skills for Experiential Learning: What Skills Do Students Need to Make the Most of Experiential Learning Opportunities?* East Lansing, MI: Michigan State University Instruction Center.

Duley, J. (1982) *Learning Outcomes: Measuring and Evaluating Experiential Learning,* PANEL resource paper 6. Raleigh, NC: NSIEE.

Edgerton, D. (1991) The prophet militant and industrial: the peculiarities of Correlli Barnett, *Twentieth Century British History,* 2(3): 360–79.

Edwards, E.G. (1982) *Higher Education for Everyone.* Nottingham, Spokesman.

Ellis, R. (ed.) (1993) *Quality Assurance for University Teaching.* Buckingham, SRHE and Open University Press.

Entwistle, N. (1992) *The Impact of Teaching on Learning Outcomes in Higher Education: a Literature Review.* Sheffield: Committee of Vice-chancellors and Principals of the Universities of the United Kingdom, Universities' Staff Development Unit.

Entwistle, N. and Marton, F. (1984) Changing conceptions of learning and research, in F. Marton, D. Hounsell and N. Entwistle (eds) *The Experience of Learning.* Edinburgh: Scottish Academic Press.

Entwistle, N. and Ramsden, P. (1983) *Understanding Student Learning.* London: Croom Helm.

Evans, N. (1981) *The Knowledge Revolution: Making the Link Between Learning and Work.* London: Grant McIntyre.

Evans, N. (1983) *Curriculum Opportunity: a Map of Experiential Learning in Entry Requirements to Higher and Further Education Award Bearing Courses,* a project report. London: Further Education Unit, Department of Education and Science.

Evans, N. (1984a) *Exploiting Experience,* FEU/PICKUP project report. London: Further Education Unit.

Evans, N. (1984b) *Access to Higher Education: Non-standard Entry to CNAA First Degree and DipHE Courses.* London: Council for National Academic Awards.

Evans, N. (1987) *Assessing Experiential Learning: a Review of Progress and Practice.* London: Longman for FEU Publications.

Evans, N. (1988) *The Assessment of Prior Experiential Learning.* London, Council for National Academic Awards.

Feldman, K.A. and Newcomb, T.M. (1969) *The Impact of College on Students.* San Francisco: Jossey-Bass.

Field, L. and Drysdale, D. (1991) *Training for Competence.* London: Kogan Page.

Finnegan, R. (1994) Recovering 'academic community': what do we mean?, in R. Barnett (ed.) *Academic Community: Discourse or Discord?* London: Jessica Kingsley.

Fletcher, S. (1991) *NVQs: Standards and Competence.* London: Kogan Page.

Frederiks, M.M.H., Westerheijden, D.F. and Weusthof, P.J.M. (1994) Effects of quality assessment in Dutch higher education, *European Journal of Higher Education,* 29(2): 181–99.

Freeman, R.B. (1976) *The Overeducated American.* New York: Academic Press.

Friedrichs, R.W. (1972) *A Sociology of Sociology.* New York: Free Press.

Further Education Unit (nd) *Aspects of Assessing Experiential Learning – Case Studies.* London: Department of Education and Science/FEU.

Gaff, J.G. (1969) *The Cluster College.* San Francisco: Jossey-Bass.

Gay, J.D. (1978) *The Christian Campus: the Role of the English Churches in Higher Education.* Abingdon: Culham College Institute.

Gibbons, M. (1993) Methods for the evaluation of research, in M. Kogan (ed.) *Evaluating Higher Education.* London: Jessica Kingsley Publishers.

Giddens, A. (1991) *Modernity and Self-identity: Self and Society in the Late Modern Age.* Cambridge: Polity Press.

Ginsberg, M. (1961) *Evolution and Progress.* London: Heinemann.

GMC (1994) *Tomorrow's Doctors.* London: General Medical Council.

Goffmann, E. (1963) *Stigma: Notes on the Management of Spoiled Identity.* Englewood Cliffs, NJ: Prentice-Hall.

Goffmann, E. (1969) *The Presentation of Self in Every-day Life.* London, Allen Lane: The Penguin Press.

Goffmann, E. (1972) *Interaction Ritual* (1967). London, Allen Lane: The Penguin Press.

Goodger, E.M. and Tilley, R.P.R. (1970) *Career Survey of Past Students, 1929–1963.* London: Imperial College.

Goodlad, S. (1970) Project work in developing countries: a British experiment in engineering education, *International Journal of Electrical Engineering Education,* 8: 135–40.

Goodlad, S. (ed.) (1975a) *Education and Social Action.* London: George Allen & Unwin.

Goodlad, S. (ed.) (1975b) *Project Methods in Higher Education.* Guildford: SRHE.

Goodlad, S. (1976) *Conflict and Consensus in Higher Education.* London: Hodder and Stoughton Educational.

Goodlad, S. (1977) *Socio-technical Projects in Engineering Education,* General Education in Engineering Project. Stirling: University of Stirling GEE Project.

Goodlad, S. (1979) *Learning by Teaching: an Introduction to Tutoring.* London: Community Service Volunteers.

Goodlad, S. (ed.) (1982) *Study Service: an Examination of Community Service as a Method of Study in Higher Education.* Windsor: NFER-Nelson.

Goodlad, S. (1983a) Contemporary collegiality: a note on institutional style and teaching method, *Higher Education Newsletter,* 6: 30–6.

Goodlad, S. (ed.) (1983b) *Economies of Scale in Higher Education.* Guildford: SRHE.

Goodlad, S. (1988) Four forms of heresy in higher education: aspects of academic freedom in education for the professions, Chapter 5 of Tight, M. (ed.) *Academic Freedom and Responsibility.* Milton Keynes: SRHE and Open University Press.

Goodlad, S. (1990a) Need mathematics and science present a problem for access to universities?, in G. Parry and C. Wake (eds) *Access and Alternative Futures for Higher Education.* London: Hodder and Stoughton.

Goodlad, S. (1990b) *Speaking Technically: a Handbook for Scientists and Engineers on How to Improve Technical Presentations.* Richmond: Goodlad.

Goodlad, S. (1992) *Undergraduate Research Opportunities Programme UROP: Report on Academic Year 1991–1992.* London: Imperial College of Science, Technology and Medicine.

Goodlad, S. and Hirst, B. (1989) *Peer Tutoring: a Guide to Learning by Teaching.* London: Kogan Page.

Goodlad, S. and Hirst, B. (eds) (1990) *Explorations in Peer Tutoring.* Oxford: Basil Blackwell.

Goodlad, S. and Hughes, J. (1992) Reflection through action: peer tutoring as service learning, in R. Barnett (ed.) *Learning to Effect.* Buckingham: SRHE and Open University Press.

Goodlad, S., Mohan, R., Shields, J. and Wield, D. (1970) The demand for non-technical studies at Imperial College, *Liberal Education,* 17: 32–7.

Goodlad, S. and Pippard, B. (1982) The curriculum of higher education, in D.A. Bligh (ed.) *Professionalism and Flexibility for Learning, Volume 6.* Leverhulme Programme of Study into the Future of Higher Education. Guildford: SRHE.

Gouldner, A.W. (1971) *The Coming Crisis of Western Sociology.* London: Heinemann Educational Books.

Grant, P. (1994) *Spiritual Discourse and the Meaning of Persons.* New York: St Martin's Press.

Green, D. (ed.) (1994) *What Is Quality in Higher Education?* Buckingham: SRHE and Open University Press.

Halsey, A.H. (1992) *The Decline of Donnish Dominion.* Oxford: Clarendon Press.

Halsey, A.H., Heath, A.F. and Ridge, J.M. (1980) *Origins and Destinations: Family, Class and Education in Modern Britain.* Oxford: Clarendon Press.

Hamilton, D., King, C., Jenkins, D., Parlett, M. and MacDonald, B. (eds) (1977) *Beyond the Numbers Game.* London: Macmillan.

Harland, J. and Gibbs, I. (1986) *Beyond Graduation.* Guildford: SRHE.

HEFCE (1993) *Description of the Template Used in June 1993 to Analyse the Self-assessments and Claims for Excellence Received in May 1993.* Bristol, Higher Education Funding Council Quality Assessment Committee: July.

Hendel, D.D. and Enright, R. (1978) An evaluation of a full-time work/study programme for undergraduates, *Alternative Higher Education,* 3.

HEQC (1993) *Request for Briefing Documentation.* Birmingham, Higher Education Quality Council Division of Quality Audit: June.

Hirsch, E.D. (1987) *Cultural Literacy: What Every American Needs to Know.* Boston: Houghton Mifflin.

Hirsch, F. (1977) *Social Limits to Growth.* London: Routledge and Kegan Paul.

Hirst, P.H. (1974) *Knowledge and the Curriculum.* London: Routledge and Kegan Paul.

Hursh, D.E. (1976) Personalized systems of instruction: what do the data indicate?, *Journal of Personalized Instruction,* 1: 91–105.

Jacob, P.E. (1957) *Changing Values in College: an Exploratory Study of the Impact of Teaching.* New York: Harper and Row.

Jessup, G. (1991) *Outcomes: NVQs and the Emerging Model of Education and Training.* London: Falmer Press.

Johnes, J. and Taylor, J. (1990) *Performance Indicators in Higher Education.* Milton Keynes: SRHE and Open University Press.

Johnston, J.M. (ed.) (1975) *Behavior Research and Technology in Higher Education.* Springfield, IL: Charles C. Thomas.

Keeton, M. and Associates (1977) *Experiential Learning: Rationale, Characteristics and Assessment.* London: Jossey-Bass.

Keller, F.S. (1968) Goodbye teacher, *Journal of Applied Behavior Analysis,* 1: 79–89.

Kerckhoff, A.C. and Trott, J.M. (1993) Educational attainment in a changing educational system: the case of England and Wales, in Y. Shavit and H. Blossfeld (eds) *Persistent Inequality: Changing Educational Attainments in 13 Countries.* Oxford: Westview Press.

Kerr, C. (1963) *The Uses of the University.* Cambridge, MA: Harvard University.

Kerr, C. and Gade, M.L. (1986) *The Many Lives of Academic Presidents.* Washington, DC: Association of Governing Boards of Universities and Colleges.

King, R. (1976) *School and College: Studies of Post-sixteen Education.* London: Routledge and Kegan Paul.

Knowles, M.S. (1986) *Using Learning Contracts.* San Francisco: Jossey-Bass.

Kuhn, T.S. (1962) *The Structure of Scientific Revolutions.* Chicago: Chicago University Press.

Kulik, J.A. and Kulik, C-L. (1976) Research on the personalized system of instruction, *Journal of Programmed Learning and Educational Technology*, 13(1): 23–30.

Kulik, J.A., Kulik, C-L. and Carmichael, K.C. (1974) The Keller Plan in science teaching: an individually paced, student-tutored, and mastery-oriented instructional method is evaluated, *Science*, 183(4123): 379–83.

Kulik, J.A., Kulik, C-L. and Cohen, P.A. (1979) A meta-analysis of outcome studies of Keller's personalized system of instruction, *American Psychologist* 34(4): 307–18.

Laurillard, D. (1979) The process of student learning, *Higher Education*, 8: 395–409.

Laurillard, D. (1987) The different forms of learning in psychology and education, in J.T.E. Richardson, M.W. Eysenck and D. Warren-Piper (eds) *Student Learning: Research in Education and Cognitive Psychology.* Milton Keynes: SRHE and Open University Press.

Leemon, T.A. (1972) *The Rites of Passage in a Student Culture: a Study of the Dynamics of Transition.* New York: Teachers College Press: Columbia University.

Locke, M., Pratt, J. and Burgess, T. (1985) *The Colleges of Higher Education 1972–1982.* Croydon: Critical Press.

Lucas, F.L. (1961) The Search for Good Sense: *Four Eighteenth Century Characters. Johnson, Chesterfield, Boswell, Goldsmith.* New York: Macmillan.

McGregor, G. (1991) *A Church College for the Twenty-First Century? 150 Years of Ripon and York St John 1841–1991.* York: William Sessions Limited for University College of Ripon and York St John.

MacIntyre, A. (1980) A crisis in moral philosophy: why is the search for the foundations of ethics so frustrating?, in H.J.T. Engelhardt and D. Callahan (eds) *Knowing and Valuing: the Search for Common Roots.* New York: The Hastings Centre.

MacIntyre, A. (1981) *After Virtue: a Study in Moral Theory.* South Bend, IN: University of Notre Dame Press.

MacIntyre, A. (1988) *Whose Justice? Which Rationality?* London: Duckworth.

MacIntyre, A. (1990) *Three Rival Versions of Moral Enquiry.* London: Duckworth.

MacVicar, M.L.A. and McGavern, N. (1984) Not only engineering: the MIT undergraduate research opportunities programme, in S. Goodlad (ed.) *Education for the Professions: Quis Custodiet?* Windsor: SRHE and NFER-Nelson.

Marris, R. (1986) Higher education and the mixed economy: the concept of competition, *Studies in Higher Education*, 11(2): 131–54.

Marton, F. (1981) Phenomenography – describing conceptions of the world around us, *Instructional Science*, 10: 177–200.

Marton, F. and Ramsden, P. (1988) What does it take to improve learning? Chapter 14 of Ramsden, P. (ed.) *Improving Learning: New Perspectives.* London: Kogan Page.

Marton, F. and Saljo, R. (1976) On qualitative differences in learning: I, outcome and process, *British Journal of Educational Psychology*, 46: 4–11.

Marton, F. and Saljo, R. (1984) Approaches to learning, in F. Marton, D. Hounsell and N. Entwistle (eds) *The Experience of Learning.* Edinburgh: Scottish Academic Press.

Meyer, J.H.F. and Muller, M.W. (1990) Evaluating the quality of student learning. I, an unfolding analysis of the association between perceptions of learning context and approaches to studying at an individual level, *Studies in Higher Education*, 15(2): 131–54.

Meyer, J.H.F. and Watson, R.M. (1991) Evaluating the quality of student learning: II, study orchestration and the curriculum, *Studies in Higher Education*, 16(3): 251–75.

Minogue, K.R. (1973) *The Concept of a University*. London, Weidenfeld and Nicolson.

Moberly, W. (1949) *The Crisis in the University*. London: SCM Press.

Moore, D. (1981) Discovering the pedagogy of experience, *Harvard Educational Review*, 51(May): 2.

Moulakis, A. (1993) *Beyond Utility: Liberal Education for a Technological Age*. London: University of Missouri Press.

Neave, G. (1994) The politics of quality: development in higher education in Western Europe 1992–1994, *European Journal of Higher Education*, 29(2): 115–34.

Neufeld, V. and Chong, J. (1984) Problem-based learning in medicine, in S. Goodlad (ed.) *Education for the Professions: Quis Custodiet?* Windsor: SRHE and NFER-Nelson.

NIACE (1989) *Adults in Higher Education: a Policy Discussion Paper*. Leicester, National Institute for Adult and Continuing Education.

Nisbet, R. (1971) *The Degradation of the Academic Dogma*. London: Heinemann Educational Books.

Nozick, R. (1974) *Anarchy, State, and Utopia*. Oxford: Basil Blackwell.

OECD (1984) *OECD Science and Technology Indicators: Resources Devoted to R & D*. Paris: Organization for Economic Co-operation and Development.

Pace, R.C. (1941) *They Went to College: a Study of 951 Former University Students*. Minneapolis: University of Minnesota Press.

Pace, R.C. (1979) *Measuring Outcomes of College: Fifty Years of Findings and Recommendations for the Future*. San Francisco: Jossey-Bass.

Parlett, M. and Dearden, G. (1977) *Introduction to Illuminative Evaluation: Studies in Higher Education*. Cardiff-by-the-Sea, CA: Pacific Soundings Press.

Pateman, T. (ed.) (1972) *Counter Course: a Handbook of Course Criticism*. Harmondsworth: Penguin.

Pelikan, J. (1992) *The Idea of the University: a Reexamination*. London: Yale University Press.

Percy, J. and Ramsden, P. (1980) *Independent Study: Two Examples from Higher Education*. Guildford: SRHE.

Perkins, J.A. (ed.) (1972) *Higher Education: from Autonomy to Systems*. New York: International Council for Educational Development.

Perry, W.G. (1970) *Forms of Intellectual and Ethical Development in the College Years: a Scheme*. New York: Holt, Rinehart and Winston.

Perry, W.G. (1981) Cognitive and ethical growth: the making of meaning, in A.W. Chickering (ed.), *The Modern American College*. San Francisco: Jossey-Bass.

Phenix, P.H. (1964) *Realms of Meaning*. New York: McGraw-Hill.

Polanyi, M. (1958) *Personal Knowledge: towards a Post-critical Philosophy*. London: Routledge and Kegan Paul.

Ramsden, P. (1987) Improving teaching and learning in higher education: the case for a relational perspective, *Studies in Higher Education*, 12(3): 275–86.

Ramsden, P. (ed.) (1988) *Improving Learning: New Perspective*. London: Kogan Page.

Ravitch, D. (1977) The revisionists revised: studies in the historiography of American education, *Proceedings of the National Academy of Education*, 4: 1–84.

Rawls, J. (1972) *A Theory of Justice*. Oxford, Clarendon Press.

Reeves, M. (1988) *The Crisis in Higher Education: Competence, Delight, and the Common Good*. Milton Keynes: SRHE and Open University Press.

Roberts, P. (1994) Creating a learning community on campus, in R. Barnett (ed.), *Academic Community: Discourse or Discord?* London: Jessica Kingsley.

Robbins Committee (1963) *Higher Education,* Committee on Higher Education, Ministry of Education. The Robbins report, Cmnd 2154. London: HMSO.

Robbins, D. (1988) *The Rise of Independent Study.* Milton Keynes: Open University Press.

Robin, A.R. (1976) Behavioral instruction in the college classroom, *Review of Educational Research,* 46(3): 313–54.

Rogers, C.R. (1969) *Freedom to Learn.* Ohio: Charles Merrill.

Rothblatt, S. (1976) *Tradition and Change in English Liberal Education.* London: Faber and Faber.

Rothblatt, S. (1933) The limbs of Osiris: liberal education in the English-speaking world, in S. Rothblatt and B. Wittrock (eds), *The European and American University Since 1800.* Cambridge: Cambridge University Press.

Rothblatt, S. and Wittrock, B. (1993) *The European and American University Since 1800.* Cambridge: Cambridge University Press.

Rowntree, D. (1988) *Educational Technology in Curriculum Development.* London, Paul Chapman Publishing.

Russell, C. (1993) *Academic Freedom.* London: Routledge.

Sartre, J-P. (1965) *Existentialism and Humanism.* London: Methuen.

Sarup, M. (1978) *Marxism and Education.* London: Routledge and Kegan Paul.

Scherer, J. (1972) *Contemporary Community: Sociological Illusion or Reality.* London: Tavistock.

Schön, D. (1983) *The Reflective Practitioner.* New York: Basic Books.

Schön, D. (1987) *Educating the Reflective Practitioner.* London: Jossey-Bass.

Schools Council (1970) *Sixth Form Survey. Volume 1, Sixth Form Pupils and Teachers.* London: Books for Schools.

Schumacher, C. (1983) The problem of scale in higher education, in S. Goodlad (ed.), *Economies of Scale in Higher Education.* Guildford: SRHE.

Schumacher, C. (1994) Creating community among teachers: a case study, in R. Barnett (ed.), *Academic Community: Discourse or Discord?* London: Jessica Kingsley.

Sear, K. (1983) Economies of scale in higher education, in S. Goodlad (ed.), *Economies of Scale in Higher Education.* Guildford: Society for Research into Higher Education.

Sharp, R. (1980) *Knowledge, Ideology, and the Politics of Schooling: towards a Marxist Analysis of Education.* London: Routledge and Kegan Paul.

Shattock, M. (1994) *The UGC and the Management of British Universities.* Buckingham: SRHE and Open University Press.

Skinner, B.F. (1968) *The Technology of Teaching.* New York: Appleton-Century-Crofts.

Skinner, B.F. (1971) *Beyond Freedom and Dignity.* New York: Alfred A. Knopf.

Skinner, J.E. (1968) College and community, *Education for Teaching,* 72: 2–15.

Smith, B. (1985) Problem-based learning: the social work experience, in D. Boud (ed.), *Problem-Based Learning in Education for the Professions.* Sydney: Higher Education Research and Development Society of Australasia.

Smith, D.M. and Saunders, M.R. (1991) *Other Routes: Part-time Higher Education Policy.* Milton Keynes: SRHE and Open University Press.

Smithers, A.G. (1976) *Sandwich Courses: an Integrated Education?* Windsor: NFER.

Squires, G. (1987) *The Curriculum Beyond School.* London: Hodder and Stoughton.

Squires, G. (1990) *First Degree: the Undergraduate Curriculum.* Milton Keynes: SRHE and Open University Press.

Stanton, T. and Ali, K. (1987) *The Experienced Hand: a Student Manual for Making the Most of Internships.* Cranston, RI: Carroll Press.

Stewart, W.A.C. (1989) *Higher Education in Postwar Britain.* London: Macmillan.

Swann Committee (1968) *The Flow into Employment of Scientists, Engineers, and Technologists,* Committee on Manpower Resources for Science and Technology, Department of Education and Science. The Swann Report, Cmnd 3760. London: HMSO.

Tapper, T. and Salter, B. (1992) *Oxford, Cambridge and the Changing Idea of the University: the Challenge to Donnish Domination.* Buckingham: SRHE and Open University Press.

Taveggia, T.L. (1976) Personalized instruction: a summary of comparative research, 1967–1974, *American Journal of Physics,* 44(11): 1028–33.

Tawney, D. (ed.) *Curriculum Evaluation Today.* London: Macmillan.

Thomas, R. and Chickering, A.W. (1983) Institutional size, higher education and student development, in S. Goodlad (ed.), *Economies of Scale in Higher Education.* Guildford: SRHE.

Tight, M. (ed.) (1988) *Academic Freedom and Responsibility.* Milton Keynes: SRHE and Open University Press.

Tight, M. (1991) *Higher Education: a Part-time Perspective.* Milton Keynes: SRHE and Open University Press.

Tiryakian, E.A. (1962) *Sociologism and Existentialism.* Englewood Cliffs, NJ: Prentice-Hall.

Tonnies, F. (1957) *Community and Society.* East Lansing: Michigan State University Press.

Trow, M. (1983) Differences between the nominal and effective sizes of higher education institutions, in S. Goodlad (ed.), *Economies of Scale in Higher Education.* Guildford: SRHE.

Trow, M. (1994) *Managerialism and the Academic Profession: Quality and Control,* Quality Support Centre Higher Education report no. 2. London: Open University.

Turner, R.H. (1961) Modes of social ascent through education: sponsored and contest mobility, in A.H. Halsey, J. Floud and C.A. Anderson (eds), *Education, Economy and Society.* New York: The Free Press.

UCCA (1989) *Statistical Supplement to the Twenty-sixth Report 1987–88.* Cheltenham: University Central Council on Admissions.

Van Gennep, A. (1960) *The Rites of Passage.* London: Routledge and Kegan Paul.

VSCC (1985) The contribution of the voluntary sector to higher education in England. A Statement, October 1985. London: Voluntary Sector Consultative Council. (The complete papers of the VSCC are held in the archives of the library of the Cheltenham and Gloucester Institute of Higher Education).

Warren-Piper, D. (ed.) (1981) *Is Higher Education Fair?* Papers presented to the 17th Annual Conference of the Society for Research into Higher Education. Guildford: SRHE.

Watson, D., Brooks, J., Coghill, C., Lindsay, R. and Scurry, D. (1989) *Managing the Modular Course: Perspectives from Oxford Polytechnic.* Milton Keynes: SRHE and Open University Press.

Webster, A. (1994) University–corporate ties and the construction of research agendas, *Sociology,* 28(1): 123–42.

Weil, S.W. and McGill, I. (eds) (1989) *Making Sense of Experiential Learning: Diversity in Theory and Practice.* Milton Keynes: SRHE and Open University Press.

Whitehead, A.N. (1932) *The Aims of Education.* London: Ernest Benn.

Whitley, P. (1980) *An Enquiry into Study Service in Institutions of Higher Education.* London: Community Service Volunteers.

Whitley, P. (1982) Study service in the United Kingdom: a survey, in S. Goodlad (ed.), *Study Service: an Examination of Community Service as a Method of Study in Higher Education.* Windsor: NFER-Nelson.

Wiener, M. (1981) *English Culture and the Decline of the Industrial Spirit 1850–1950.* Cambridge: Cambridge University Press.

Willingham, W.W. (1977) *Principles of Good Practice in Assessing Experiential Learning.* Columbia, MD: CAEL.

Woodley, A., Wagner, L., Slowey, M., Hamilton, M. and Fulton, O. (1987) *Choosing to Learn: Adults in Education.* London: SRHE and Open University Press.

Wooldridge, A. (1994) Universities: towers of babble, *The Economist,* 25 December 1993 to 7 January 1994: 54–6.

Wyatt, J.F. (1977a) The idea of community in institutions of higher education, *Studies in Higher Education,* 2(2): 125–35.

Wyatt, J.F. (1977b) 'Collegiality' during a period of rapid change in higher education: an examination of a distinctive feature claimed by a group of colleges of education in the 1960s and 1970s, *Oxford Review of Education,* 3(2): 147–55.

Yelon, S.L. and Duley, J.S. (1978) *Efficient Evaluation of Individual Performance in Field Placements,* Guides for the Improvement of Instruction in Higher Education 14. East Lansing: Michigan State University Instructional Media Center.

Young, M.F.D. (ed.) (1971) *Knowledge and Control: New Directions for the Sociology of Education.* London: Collier-Macmillan.

Index

The Society for Research into Higher Education

The Society for Research into Higher Education exists to stimulate and co-ordinate research into all aspects of higher education. It aims to improve the quality of higher education through the encouragement of debate and publication on issues of policy, on the organization and management of higher education institutions, and on the curriculum and teaching methods.

The Society's income is derived from subscriptions, sales of its books and journals, conference fees and grants. It receives no subsidies, and is wholly independent. Its individual members include teachers, researchers, managers and students. Its corporate members are institutions of higher education, research institutes, professional, industrial and governmental bodies. Members are not only from the UK, but from elsewhere in Europe, from America, Canada and Australasia, and it regards its international work as amongst its most important activities.

Under the imprint *SRHE & Open University Press*, the Society is a specialist publisher of research, having some 45 titles in print. The Editorial Board of the Society's Imprint seeks authoritative research or study in the above fields. It offers competitive royalties, a highly recognizable format in both hardback and paperback and the world-wide reputation of the Open University Press.

The Society also publishes *Studies in Higher Education* (three times a year), which is mainly concerned with academic issues, *Higher Education Quarterly* (formerly *Universities Quarterly*), mainly concerned with policy issues, *Research into Higher Education Abstracts* (three times a year), and *SRHE News* (four times a year).

The Society holds a major annual conference in December, jointly with an institution of higher education. In 1992, the topic was 'Learning to Effect', with Nottingham Trent University. In 1993, it was 'Governments and the Higher Education Curriculum: Evolving Partnerships' at the University of Sussex in Brighton, and in 1994 'The Student Experience' at the University of York. Future conferences include in 1995, 'The Changing University' at Heriot-Watt University in Edinburgh.

The Society's committees, study groups and branches are run by the members. The groups at present include:
Teacher Education Study Group
Continuing Education Group
Staff Development Group
Excellence in Teaching and Learning

Benefits to members

Individual

Individual members receive:

- *SRHE News*, the Society's publications list, conference details and other material included in mailings.
- Greatly reduced rates for *Studies in Higher Education* and *Higher Education Quarterly*.
- A 35% discount on all Open University Press & SRHE publications.
- Free copies of the Precedings – commissioned papers on the theme of the Annual Conference.
- Free copies of *Research into Higher Education Abstracts*.
- Reduced rates for conferences.
- Extensive contacts and scope for facilitating initiatives.
- Reduced reciprocal memberships.

Corporate

Corporate members receive:

- All benefits of individual members, plus
- Free copies of *Studies in Higher Education*.
- Unlimited copies of the Society's publications at reduced rates.
- Special rates for its members e.g. to the Annual Conference.

Membership details: SRHE, 3 Devonshire Street, London,
W1N 2BA, UK. Tel: 0171 637 2766
Catalogue: SRHE & Open University Press, Celtic Court,
22 Ballmoor, Buckingham MK18 1XW. Tel: (01280) 823388

WHAT IS QUALITY IN HIGHER EDUCATION?

Diana Green (ed.)

In the UK, the absence of any agreed definition of quality is problematic in the wake of the changes set in train by the 1988 Education Reform Act. Pressure for greater accountability in the use of public funds and changes to the structure and funding of higher education (designed to increase competition for students and resources) provided the initial rationale for giving quality a higher profile than in the past. The Government's commitment to a higher participation rate, together with the decision to overtly tie quality assessment to funding decisions, sharpened the concern. However, a fundamental dilemma remains: if there is no consensus about what quality is in higher education, how can it be assessed?

This book was stimulated by, and reflects some of the debate following the publication of the 1991 Further and Higher Education Bill and its subsequent enactment. It also draws on the preliminary findings of a major national research project funded by a partnership of government, business and higher education, designed to develop and test methods for systematically assessing quality.

The focus here is on the quality of teaching and learning. The book illustrates the extent to which quality has overtaken efficiency as the key challenge facing higher education in the 1990s. It underlines the growing awareness that institutions are accountable not only to the government which funds them but also, in an increasingly competitive higher education market, to the customers – the students. The book therefore signals the early stages of what threatens to be a cultural revolution as profound as that which has transformed the behaviour of organizations in the manufacturing and commercial sectors.

Contents
Part 1: What is quality in higher education? – Concepts, policy and practice – Quality in higher education: a funding council perspective – Part 2: Models from within British higher education – Defining and measuring the quality of teaching – Inspecting quality in the classroom: an HMI perspective – Quality audit in the universities – Part 3: Models from beyond British higher education – Quality and its measurement: a business perspective – Royal Mail: developing a total quality organization – Quality in higher education: an international perspective – Looking ahead – Index.

Contributors
Jim Finch, Malcolm Frazer, Diana Green, Terry Melia, Baroness Pauline Perry, Ian Raisbeck, William H. Stubbs, Carole Webb.

160pp   0 335 15740 8 (Paperback)   0 335 15741 6 (Hardback)

QUALITY ASSURANCE FOR UNIVERSITY TEACHING

Roger Ellis (ed.)

Assuring quality for teaching in a time of rapid change is the major challenge facing UK universities. This informative and practical book combines review chapters with case studies within a number of comparative perspectives. The book is organized around three themes. First there are descriptions of approaches to quality assurance. These include case studies from universities of TQM and BS 5750, course validation and review, student evaluation and institutional research, together with reviews of relevant approaches from industry and health care. Quality assurance based on professionalism is also considered. Second, the characteristics of quality teaching are addressed including summaries of research evidence, the results of a unique participant study, standards generated by quality circles of staff and students and a description of distinguished teaching awards in the UK and USA. Third, approaches to the development of university teachers are covered including teaching training, staff development, appraisal and the enterprise initiative.

Contents
Part 1: Assuring quality – Quality assurance for university teaching: issues and approaches – A British Standard for university teaching? – Total quality management through BS 5750: a case study – Quality assurance in health care: the implications for university teaching – Quality assurance through course validation and review – Assuring quality through student evaluation – Institutional research and quality assurance – University teaching: a professional model for quality – Part 2: Identifying quality – Teaching styles of award-winning professors – The first distinguished teaching award in the United Kingdom – Expert teachers' perceptions of university teaching: the identification of teaching skills – Teaching standards from quality circles – Effective teaching – Part 3: Developing quality – Appraisal schemes and their contribution to quality in teaching – Staff development and quality assurance – Teacher training for university teachers? – Quality in teaching and the encouragement of enterprise – Glossary – Indexes.

Contributors
Jennifer Boore, George Brown, John Dallat, Roger Ellis, Lewis Elton, Catherine Finlay, Norman Gibson, Sandra Griffiths, Jerry M. Lewis, Saranne Magennis, Gordon Rae, Christine Saunders, Eric Saunders, Susan Storey, Maurice Stringer, Ann Tate, Elaine Thomas, Dorothy Whittington, Roger Woodward.

336pp   0 335 19025 1 (Paperback)   0 335 19026 X (Hardback)

THE LIMITS OF COMPETENCE
KNOWLEDGE, HIGHER EDUCATION AND SOCIETY

Ronald Barnett

Competence is a term which is making its entrance in the university. How might it be understood at this level? *The Limits of Competence* takes an uncompromising line, providing a sustained critique of the notion of competence as wholly inadequate for higher education.

Currently, we are seeing the displacement of one limited version of competence by another even more limited interpretation. In the older definition – one of academic competence – notions of disciplines, objectivity and truth have been central. In the new version, competence is given an operational twist and is marked out by know-how, competence and skills. In this operationalism, the key question is not 'What do students understand?' but 'What can students do?'

The book develops an alternative view, suggesting that, for our universities, a third and heretical conception of human being is worth considering. Our curricula might, instead, offer an education for life.

Contents

Introduction – Part 1: Knowledge, higher education and society: The learning society? – A certain way of knowing? – We are all clerks now – Part 2: The new vocabulary: 'Skills' and 'vocationalism' – 'Competence' and 'outcomes' – 'Capability' and 'enterprise' – Part 3: The lost vocabulary: Understanding – Critique – Interdisciplinarity – Wisdom – Part 4: Competence reconsidered: Two rival versions of competence – Beyond competence – Retrospect and coda – Bibliography – Index.

224pp   0 335 19341 2 (Paperback)   0 335 19070 7 (Hardback)